A DOODLING
NOODLING BRAIN

T0078334

A DOODLING NOODLING BRAIN

or

How to Prevent ALZHEIMER'S

**Collection of Humorous
and Thought Provoking
Short stories-Poems-Limericks
&
Brain Doodles**

Lyn Rafe-Lawyer

To order additional copies of this book, contact:
Xlibris LLC
1-888-795-4274
www.Xlibris.com
Orders@Xlibris.com
551455

CONTENTS

DOODLES

POETRY

POETRY

continued

POETRY

continued

LIMERICKS

HOMONYMS

SHORT STORIES

DEDICATED
to
My beautiful and beloved
only sibling
Irene Joan Rolph
aka
The Dutchiss of Fulbourn
1924-2007

Please note: My many references to 'poor as church mice' parents and the experiences of WW II
are purposeful; inspite of enormous tribulations my sister and I inherited the abundant spiritual riches of patience, honesty and integrity from our beloved parents.

PROLOGUE

At this late stage of my life
analogous to a nagging wife
thoughts in my brain
keep pounding like rain
joys, tribulations and strife

A catharsis is no mystery
all possess our own history
Experiences inane and exciting
gave impetus to this tribe scribe
to keep on writing

Whether you agree or
disagree with me
I'm grateful for
the possibility
you took the time
to read my prose and rhyme
and ignored
video games and TV

about the author

Lyn Rafe-Lawyer was born in London, England and left her beloved country in 1952 at age nineteen to pursue the American Dream.

A survivor of World War 11, breast cancer and now legally blind, Lyn has led an extraordinary life and career.

An activist, inventor, creator of Miami Advice Advertising & Public Relations Agency—Pantunics Elegant Casual Clothing and a published ABSOLUT artist.

**Lyn's mission is to improve products and services for Seniors, the visually impaired,
the disabled and rescue abused children and animals.**

Lyn Rafe-Lawyer Book Collection

KEEP YOUR PECKER UP—an endearing Cockney epithet synonymous with courage portrays a hundred year saga of Lyn's English family concluding with World War Two and Lyn's immigration to the United States of America.

BRIEF ENCOUNTERS—A 21st Century Canterbury Tale, a continuum of Keep Your Pecker Up is Lyn's personal pilgrimage in pursuit of the American Dream burnished with humour and adventure.

LYN'S ASS LEGACY—Twenty-two humorous cartoons dispel disrespect for the inaptly named lowly, hard working Donkey.

PARTY ANIMAL CHIT CHAT—Forty-four pages of Lyn's humorous drawings and captions of her beloved animals, birds and fish having a conversational ball and a collection of Lyn's charming annual greetings.

Read excerpts & review video
www.lynrafe-lawyer.com

DELIGHTFUL CHILDREN'S LITERATURE

by
Lyn Rafe-Lawyer
available by contacting
Telephone—954 455 0928

THE EASTER BUNNY'S SAD TALE OF WOE AND WHY HIS EARS ARE SO LONG AND DROPPY

An easy to perform one act play
for children that teaches
the essence of
good manners, humour and love.

BENJAMIN THE PEGUIN

A delightful children's short story
about an adventuresome Penguin who
becomes a star at an Ocean Aquarium.

DOODLES

okey dokey if you
find them hokey
I challenge you
to write your own
More fun than waiting
for the approval
of your bank loan
conversing with
a gnome
or if
you're a dog
chewing the fat on
your cel-bone

To amuse you
Alternate Book, Movie,
Television & Song Titles

BOOKS

The Old Maid and the Flea
(Her weapon—Lysol)

For Whom the Belles Toiled
(The Pimp and Pauper)

The Bun Also Rises
(History of Yeast Infections)

69 Shades of Paint
(Sensuous Decorating Tips)

Atlas Bugged
(CIA Conspiracy)

How To Win Friends
& Scam Influential People
(The Maydoff Debacle)

MOVIES

An American in Hialeah

**The Man in the
Grey Flannel Suite**

**Deep Croak
Kermit and Miss Piggy's
torrid love affair**

Seven Year Bitch

**Twelve Angry Men
Women and Children
stalled in elevator**

**Lost At Sea World
A Fishy Mystery**

From Hear to Senility

**Seven Brides for the
Smothers Brothers**

It's A Wonderful Life
If you have money

The Postman Never
Knocks Twice
Deadbeat Mail Carriers

Ya Wanna Pay
My Fare Lady?
Impatient cab driver

Rear Window
Colonoscopies revealed

Birth of a Station

BATMAN
My life in the sweaty dugout

The Indivisible Man

Citizen Candy Kane

Indiana Bones
Midwest Archaeology Dig

A Star is Bored
with her leading man

Shakespeare in Shock
Playwright's Casino debt

The Way We Weren't

I'll Cry Tomorrow
and Forever

Gone With the Windpipe

Around the World in 80 Daze

The Roman Spring
of a Stoned Missus

Moby Dick P.I.

Who's Afraid of Virgin Wolves?

**Breakfast at Tiffany's
Dinner McDonalds**

**Mr. Smith Goes to Washington
and is Royally Screwed**

**Saturday Night Fever
Sunday the Flu**

**Bonnie and Clydesdales
hoof it on Broadway**

Dr. Chicago

SONGS

I Get A Kick Out Of You
& it hurts

I Left My Lunch
In San Francisco

That's Why The Lady
Is A Trampoline

I Can See Cleary Now
with my new glasses

I Loves Ya Porky
on rye with mustard

Rudy the Red nosed
Doorman

Getting To Know You
is expensive

**Oh What A
Beautiful Mourning
Cowboy's lament**

**I'm Dreaming of a
White House
Dinner Invitation**

**Climb Every Mountain
except Everest**

**When Irish IRA's
Are Conspiring**

**What I Did For Love
is too disgusting to relate**

Give My Leotards To Broadway

**Pack Up Your Troubles
Kick The Old Bag Out
and Smile Smile Smile**

TELEVISION

Desperate Houseflies

American Idle

60 Minuets
Musical Version

Dateline—Frontline—Nightline
Dating—Escort Documentary

Dr. Pill—Dr. Ozzie Harriet
Judge Judy. Judy, Judy

Wheel of Fortune Cookies

Saturday Night Live or Dead

Oprah On Her Own

The View from the
Tower of Babble

Locked Up with a Broad

Happy Days in the Caves

Two and Half Idiots

Family Ties Up Traffic

The Brady Brunch

Downtown Lobby

Master Bait Theatre

ANCIENT HISTORY

ADAM sayeth to EVE
'These fig leaves giveth me hives'

NOAH
'Singing in the rain is a movie?'

MOSES
'Parting is such sweet sorrow'

CLEOPATRA
Surveyor of Rome
'Your building permits
are antiquated'

BATH SHEBA
'No Dave, I'll jump in the shower'

THOR
'A bolt of linen please'

RICHARD the 3rd
'A horse, my kingdom for a horse'
(court jester)
'Majesty are you nuts giving up
castle, moat, suppers that bloat
for a horse who prefers to
chew hay all day than run
around a royal race course?'

TROJAN
to son Promiscuous
'Don't ever forget your protection'

HELEN of TROY
'Don't tell me to get off
my high horse!'

KING TUT
to parking valet
'Toot and Car Come'

MARK ANTHONY'
'Friends Romans Countrymen
lend me your ears
(heckler)
'Okay here's mine but your message
I'm unable to hear'

CHURCHILL
'On land, sea and in the air
we shall nevah, nevah withdraw'
(his cigar)

PAUL REVERE
'The British are coming
get out the silver tea service'

LADY MACBETH
**'Should have bought Shot It Out
to remove that damn spot'**

LEWIS TO CLARKE
**'What do you mean you lost
your GPS?'**

DOCTOR, KINDEY STONE
I PRESUME!

LAWRENCE OF ARABIA
'I'd walk a mile for a Camel'

**and the
OSCAR
goes to
Oscar Myer Weenies**

NOSTRADAMUS

disguised despotic names

castrating	Castro
gobbles	Goebbels
specious spear	Speer
killer	Himmler
insane	Hussein
bastard	Bashar Assad
persecutor	Peron
ding dong dung	Kim Jong Un
fiddler fiery	Nero
calculating	Caligula
heinous	Herod
hungry one	Attila the Hun
sickle & hammer	Stalin
medical menace	Mengele
dodgy	Doge

DISCARDED HEADLINES

**The Queen's Jubilee Diamond
STOLEN**

**Eleanor Discovers FDR's Affair
'Franklin my dear
I don't give a damn'**

Betray Us with a Broad

**Sex is an itch
that has to be scratched**

**Men who think with their penis
think they are genius**

The Rising Son Moons
Venus Over Miami

Winston Tastes Good
like a Prime Minister Should

You're in Safe Hands at
State Farm
but stay away from
the mad cow pastures

The State of the Union Address
has the wrong zip code

Putin on the Ritz Cracker
'Soak 'em in vodka'

No More Kadiffi

NEVER TRY THE FOLLOWING

COFFEE ENEMAS
**good until the last drop
then all hell breaks loose**

SWIM WITH
ANDERSON COOPER

FLOAT DOWN THE
AMAZON
ON A RUBBEER TIRE

CONTACT OPRAH

ARGUE WITH DR. PHIL

XTRA XTRA
from my X Files
words to stimulate your brain
get you fired up to write, incite, inspire
create a poem, limerick or trivia

is it a lizard, gizzard.
blizzard or hazard?
a ping or pong
a melody or song
Sting, Bing, sing
a slash, bash, lash or mash
rhyme, dime, slime, thyme
soot, foot, absolute
above, love, dove
coo, woo, moo and sue
blush, flush, mush
bore, snore no more
maze, daze, glaze
dinky, slinky, kinky
sly, why, bye bye
maim, blame, claim
fiddle dee, fa la la, do re me
rosy, posy, nosy, mosey
tricky Dickey, prickly Mickey
bon jour, bon soir, bonfire, bon bon

so get cracking
have tons of fun
and don't forget to hug
your honey bun

CLICHÉS

Clichés charming and often alarming

Silence is golden
(if you're deaf)

Money doesn't grow on trees
(yes it does if you own an orchard)

All good things must come to an end
(when you're dead)

One door closes another opens
(if it isn't locked)

A pot of gold at the
rainbow's end
and you'll spend
a fortune digging it out

Look for the silver lining
(not at my cheap tailor's)

Smile and the whole
world smiles with you
(especially if you're toothless)

Ignorance is bliss
(until you read Freud)

Patience is a virtue
(at the emergency room)

The sun will come out tomorrow
(not if you live in London)

It's always darkest before dawn
(pay your electric bill)

There's no place like home
(if you're homeless)

The black sheep of the family
(better than flaming pink)

Keep your nose clean
(no Kleenex—use your sleeve)

You can lead a horse to water
but you can't make him drink
(whoever said that never
met a thirsty horse)

Honesty is the best policy
(check that one with
your insurance agent)

The grass is always greener
on the other side
(especially if you have Astro Turf)

Don't let the left hand know
what the right hand is doing
(try explaining that one
to your mother)

Don't let them see you sweat
(again explain that to your Mom!)

You can fool some of the people
some of the time
(especially if they are drunk)

There's no time like the present
(okay so where's my present?)

HOUSEHOLD NAMES IN VAIN
why I was kicked off the Spelling Bee's Team

Winston Churchill Downs
Laddie Gag Gag
Mitt Romulus
Tom Cruising
Julia Childish
David Lettercarrier
Lindsey Lowdown
Simon Coward
Mad Donna
Regis Philibuster
O.J. Simpleton
Brush Limbowwow
Billy Grahamcrackers
Benjamin Netatyahoo
Jimmy Kibblesanbits
Ellen Generous
Jessie Venturesome
Phoney Express
Walter Klondike
Llama Dahling

WHATEVER HAPPENED TO WHAT'S HIS NAME?

We all struggle to remember names of cousins, friends, the Seven Dwarfs and icons. A familiar face appears on television and the name escapes your memory. On the tip of your tongue, forehead slapping won't release the annoyance. Finally, someone utters a clue and you slap your knee issuing with a sigh, the ubiquitous 'Of course!'

Nicknames seem to help. I have two bald headed male friends, one I call Baldini and the other, the Hairless Wonder. Although my sister never forgot my name she had plenty of nicknames for me. As a child I was known as the 'little horror', teen years, 'Wreck of the Hesperus'. Blossoming into sophistication she called me, Lady Jane Grey.

Remembering famous lines often helps, for instant, 'It's going to be a bumpy ride!'—Bette Davis and 'Judy, Judy, Judy'—Cary Grant.'. Guess who said, 'Frankly my dear I don't give a damn!'—Rhett Butler or Clark Gable?

Next time you are stuck on the Seven Dwarves, here they are:

> BASHFUL
> DOC
> DOPEY
> GRUMPY
> HAPPY
> SLEEPY
> SNEEZY

NAMES YOU WILL NEVER FORGET

Anna Gramm	Author
Fran Chise	Waitress I Hop
Eddy Fiss	Architect
Claire Voyant	Psychiatrist
Jim Nast	Athlete
Steve Adoor	Dock Worker
Harry Karry	Sword swallower
Sonny Daze	Meteorologist
Kay Rashen	Food Inspector
Phil Anderer	Sex Therapist

Liz Ards	Plant Purveyor
Ellie Fant	Safari Consultant
Meg Atron	Weapons Expert
Corrie Aander	Botanist
Max Emum	Pawn Broker
Justin Thyme	Airline Pilot
Ruth Less	Attorney
Rhett Orick	Politician
Al Armist	Astrologist
Tim Idlee	Pet Groomer
Les Izmor	Dietician
Bea Hinds	Debt Collector

Bobbie Sox	Podiatrist
Peter Pekker	Urologist
Pearl White	Dentist
Dee Lishus	Chef
Albert Hall	Usher
Jay Walker	Traffic Cop
Ray Deator	Energy Expert
Rosie Hugh	House Painter
John Quill	Florist
Sally Forth	Tour Guide
Annie Mossity	Lobbyist
Rob Berry	Detective

I. Seymour	Optician
Paige Turner	Librarian
Belle Ringer	Boxing Umpire
Pattie Kake	Baker
Donna Hatt	Hairdresser
Tommy Gunn	Loan Shark
Pat Downs	Security Guard
Chris Pierre	Speech Therapist
Olive Pitts	Bartender
Percy Veer	Personal Trainer

AVOID THESE
ARRESTING ALIASES
&
OBTUSE OCCUPATIONS
when arrested crossing state lines

Al Abama
Distant cousin to Obama

Al Aska
Dogsled Musher

Ari Zona
Cactus collector

Carolina North
I invented the Charleston

Carolina South
Civil War Historian

Flo Rida
Hurricane Hunter

**Georgia
Stripper at the
KKK Klub**

**Ida Ho
Chinese chef**

**Ken Tucky
Chicken Farmer**

**Louis Iana
Damn Engineer**

**Mary Land
Oyster shucker**

**Minnie Sota
Aide to General Mills
at Pillsbury Military Academy**

Miss Isis Sippi
Egyptologist

Miss Ouri
Beauty Queen

Mitch Igan
Auto mechanic

Rhoda Island
Rhodes scholar

Tennessee Williams
I'm a cool cat on a
hot tin roof

Tex Ass
Cowboy

Virginia West
Coal miner's daughter

D.C. Washington
Monument Designer

OFF MY ROCKER

I have been certified perfectly sane except
when it comes to rocks and rockers.

'Rockers' the perpetrators of noise not
the sweet, squeaking rhythm of a wooden
rocking chair on a porch where one sits to
chat and sip a mint julep.

I am rebelling against the explosion of
'rock 'n roll'. The Rocker who stomps on
stage screaming into a mike—that means you
Mick Jagger you are not my rocker—so get
your rocks off on another planet. Remember,
a Rolling Stone bothers Kate Moss.

Not only on stage, the noise surrounds us
permeating the airwaves, radio, television,
telephone, airports, super markets, elevators
and the doctor's office.

Quote from Shakespeare's new play,
                'Rocky Road'
"Be off rocker for thou music hath no charm.
Forsooth Lady Gag Gag get ye to a monastery."

The sweet sounds of jazz; Earl 'Fatha'Hines,
Enroll Garner, Ramsey Lewis and Dave
Brubeck have disappeared. The magic of
Irving Berlin, Cole Porter, Jerome Kern,
Gershwin, Jerry Herman, Rogers and
 Hammerstein have been ignored by the
tuneless guitar-drum saturated nasal rockers.

The missing link; incomparable composers
from whom we derived our 'modern' music;
 Mozart, Puccini, Verdi, Debussy, Chopin and
Rachmaninoff are foreign words to children
of the electronic age and the tip of their inane
ignorant iceberg sinking the ship of
memorable, soaring, enchanting melodies.

BETWEEN A ROCK
AND
A HARD PLACE

The stoned perpetrator of sexual innuendo
"Getting his rocks off" insulted The Rock of
Gibraltar, Mount Everest and Rock of Ages.

POETRY

Beginning with three dissertations
voicing my opinion about
three powerful entities
radically influencing our lives
Radio, Television and Movies

There is no escape from the cacophony of
crashing, thrashing drums, screeching
guitars and explosions
imposed upon movie audiences
and television viewers

Monotonous, repetitive noise is employed
in almost every commercial, documentary
and program promotion.

There are those who have the audacity
to call the irritating noise, 'music'!
It would give me great pleasure to shove
those idiotic heads into a tuba

Extraordinarily loud audio
sound effects accompanying visuals
are deliberate—forcing immediate
body and brain reaction, stimulation
and severe hearing loss

ALL QUIET
ON THE WESTERN FRONT

A moment in time
silence was golden
The roar subsided
not a word spoken

World War One
and Two were over
Humans relaxed
and breathed easier

Freedom rang out
loud and clear
An optimistic nation
began to appear

Capturing our
senses gleefully
mesmerizing magical
bewitching TV

Madison Avenue
microscopically
studied our
innocence statistically

From tiny box
to super size
the grey glass eye
materialized

Commercial jingles
light and cheery
abruptly changed to
sounds of blurry fury

Our western front
no longer quiet
airwaves bombarded
a babbling riot

Twenty-four seven
we are inundated
repetitious messages
annoying and hated

Throbbing drums
screeching guitars
sell news, food, drugs,
sleek new cars

Television unquestionably
communicates globally
educating exponentially
science, cultures and history

My viewing habits are selective
shunning icon hype
pundits and those
excessively talkative

Attention creators of TV crap
in a flash my thumb can tap
mute on remote
and voila—instant zap

RAPPING UP AMERICA

Bombarding airwaves day and night
Blasting eardrums and our sight
Crashing cymbals explosive noises
Ah utopia say convincing voices
Rid yourself of all your ills
Take over the counter magic pills

Health beauty and success
Side affects maybe death
Lower cholesterol whiten teeth
Aching bones get relief
Seconds pass you're brand new
Depression now a rosy hue

Heartburn allergies constipation
Vanish gone no consternation
All you guys take Viagra
Erections mightier than Niagara
A lizard speaks with assurance
Make sure you buy his insurance

The friendly bear loves his ass
Uses Charmin not the grass
New car now not next year
Shout It Out stains disappear
Hire the attorney with an expansive grin
He'll get you out of the mess you're in

Swap your husband swap your wife
Cheerios extend your life
Just the tip of the commercial iceberg
Want to stop the surging surge?
Hit the mute on your remote
Bravo brave David
Goliath you hath smote

CRASHING BORES

If you haven't been annoyed
by radio, movie, television noise
Are you deaf or disinterested
knowing how our lives are manipulated?

Who has the right
to assault our airwaves
day and night?
Obviously not a meek, mild mite

Who's behind the
absurd mentality
void of originality
plaguing unrelentingly?

In ancient times drums
warned of impending gloom
Now they reverberate
in every room

Hearing loss
is at an all time high
Remember your lover's sigh
as gentle sounds fade and die

SITCOMS SOAPS TALK SHOWS

Screaming audiences applaud
at anything even when bored
A self indulgent 'me' society
they live their lives vicariously
through the 4th Estate's publicity
Magazines, radio and television
fuel a delusional imagination
Scandals and gossip they adore
whether icon or girl next door
Hooked on beauty, sexual passion
and Lady Ga Ga's outrageous fashion
Desperate housewives
Bel Aire and New Jersey
movie stars and plastic surgery
Baby bumps, marriages, divorces
famous violent domestic abuses
The endless babble of monotony
monogamy versus adultery
Trying to solve the mystery
of fragile human idolatry
I've come to the conclusion
it's a media escape from
their own reality

NOW FOR THE GOOD NEWS

I turned on my
television set
Goosebumps rose
on my face and neck
Thank God I haven't
lost my hearing yet
A crystal sound pure as gold
rang out sweet and bold
Am angelic voice
issued from a
twelve year old
Her stage presence
cool and calm
bathed the audience
with a soothing balm
Jackie Evanco
is her name
destined for stardom
and well deserved fame

FUN FOOLISHNESS

Hollywood's heyday
produced Lillian Gish
Hagen Daz ice-cream is delish
and so is my dear
beautiful girlfriend
named Trish
All babies sweetly
speak gibberish
while their siblings make
a fervent wish
for that special toy
on Santa's list
Oregon fishermen
angle for fish
Television chefs show
off a new dish
Mountaineers avoid
an icy abyss
Surgeons remove a
cancerous cyst
Stock brokers take
an enormous risk
Attorney's finger point
and insist

Used car salesmen
cajole and persist
Alcoholics enjoy
getting pissed
and remorseful at
opportunities missed
Political candidates
grinding out their
rhetoric grist
annoyed by hecklers
they try to resist
Lovers enveloped in
euphoric bliss
oblivious in their
mythical mist
not caring who
sees them kiss
Waitresses hate
to be called Miss
will place your order
on a precipice

I derived pleasure
from writing this
however, I am remiss
not disclosing
my own foolishness

ARE YOU A STAR?

Twinkle twinkle, little star
now I know what you are
dangerous gaseous hot and cold
uninhabitable so we're told

Science claim that we are
a product of a distant star
embedded with its molecules
governed by unfathomable rules

Whatever happened to Adam's rib?
was it just a legendary fib?
When we die and return to dust
into the universe are we thrust?

And the rockets red glare
speed us beyond our atmosphere
past the moon's dusty lair
Is our flag still there?

Inexplicable infinity
black holes and black energy
an unsolvable mystery
a puzzle from here to eternity

Galaxies strewn across the Universe
outnumber grains of sand on earth
planets we cannot understand
on which one will we land?

Proving a beginning and an end
an unimaginable challenge
no human brain can comprehend
Is there an answer from an alien friend?

The deeper we probe into outer space
who will win the universal race?
Will our Creator reward with grace
those invading His home base?

I'm a grateful passenger
on spaceship Earth
home of my species
place of my birth

So continue to twinkle little star
millions of miles from where we are
lighting up the sky so bright
wondrous jewel suspended in flight

WHAT KIND OF FOOL AM I?

I've never seen a UFO
suddenly appear and swiftly go
its twinkling lights all aglow
racing across the earth's sky
suspended in space miles high
Is it reverse engineering
officialdom is not revealing?
Or are they visitors
from another planet
anxious to shop 'til
they drop at Target?
Those who claim
they've been abducted
was it a fantasy
or were they instructed
to inform the human race
others exist in outer space?
So many questions unanswerable
sceptics say it's a lot of 'bull'
Then on the other hand
won't we be surprised
when 'they' land
Received with big parade
and marching band?
Then all will admit
'What kind of fool I am?

BEAM ME UP HOUDINI

Before Houdini's demise
a secret word he cleverly devised
informing his wife he had arrived
intact on the 'other side'
Years passed as she waited in vain
for the secret word that never came
Embarrassed, who was to blame?
A Houdini trick she could not explain

WHEELS OF MISFORTUNE

First time you fall off your bike
you're told to get back on
and try again
okay idiotic parents but
I'm the one sustaining pain

STUMPED

Skinny dipping is for chumps
in a murky pond with
lumps and bumps
and without your swimming trunks
be careful you don't catch
your you know what on a
dead tree stump

WE ARE NOT ALONE

**I am passionate about the other travellers on
Planet Earth
namely the animals, mammals,
birds, fish, reptiles and insects
vital to our existence
All these endearing creatures have
my utmost respect and protection**

**I could write volumes from A to Z on all
the creatures of land, air, and sea
so I've chosen a few for your review
praying you'll respect and protect
these creatures the same as me**

**THE MISSING LINK
GRATITUDE
BEES
SHAMEFUL GAMES
DANGERS OF THE DEEP
BIG AL
MY FUNNY FURRY VALENTINE
FOR THE BIRDS
HOLY COW& Short Story Explanation**

THE MISSING LINK

It remains a mystery
did our species crawl
out of slime or the sea?
Determining our
complex psyche
Is our ancestor really
a monkey?
Ironically, it's a dichotomy
studying human history
non human species
displayed far more dignity

Beloved creatures of
land, sea and air
we've shamefully
neglected your welfare
with arrogance and cruelty
with no regard for your sanctity
slaughtering you unmercifully

And there is no excuse
for us not preventing
your unrelenting abuse
We must conclude
our barbaric attitude
and preserve our precious gift
with protection, respect and
above all 'gratitude'

GRATITUDE

You may not be fans
of every species that spans
the air, sea and land
The nourishment they provided
we have decimated and divided
creating a problem we can't undo
Take a moment to think
dwell on the word 'extinct'
then please read my review

Without honey bees,
no flowers fruit and trees
No silkworms no silk
No cows no milk
cream butter or cheese
They are part of the chain
from which we humans obtain
food for our body and brain
We cannot neglect we must protect
all creatures great and small
then you'll realize
without this precious prize
we would not exist at all

BEES

My affection for the Honey Bee
limitless as the deep blue sea
with gratitude for its legacy
Tirelessly buzzing flower to flower
gathering its sweet nectar
a bountiful cargo of vital` power
Bumble Bees and their Honey
more valuable than
oil, silver, gold and money
Honey a superlative food
wondrous properties
a golden gift of ultimate good
Returning to the hive
bees convert their coveted prize
building a waxy bee hi-rise
An aloof Queen on her throne
ignores the hard work drone
building her Royal honeycomb
Now Bee news most shocking
Our precious bees are disappearing
A situation scientists find alarming
It's imperative bees stay alive
without their pollination drive
agriculture cannot survive

I beg you please
pray hard to save
our precious bees

PANDAMOANIUM

The most adored,
elusive animal
in the zoo
worries each day
'Where's my bamboo?'
It shouldn't come
as a surprise
if you were bamboozled
you too would sport
black rings
under your eyes
The moral of this message is
Leave the Pandas
to their own biz
Don't ex- or import
these unique creatures
with their exquisite features
Let them roam in
their natural habitat
to chew plentiful bamboo
and enjoy Panda chit chat

SHAMEFUL GAMES

Coliseum rings with
shouts jeers and cheers
urging warrior slaves to appear
and kill with bare hands and spears
enraged lions, tigers and bears
for whom the spectators
show no remorse or spilled tears

The crowds yelling
ole in Spain
don't give a damn
for the pain
reserved for the bull
a matador's raging tool
The Toreador's aim
adoration and fame
Excitement expands
as blood spills on sand
the brave bull
withstands his last stand

Tally Ho
the fox hunt begins
barking dogs, horses and gin
indulging those in
the vanity of sin
The poor fox in the field
unaware he's to be killed
now a nervous wreck
never knowing his fur will
adorn a dowager's neck

Safari at dawn
no sirens will warn
unarmed prey
big game hunters
are on their way
to stalk and slay
Puffed up with pride
the hunter's smile is wide
his booted foot resting leisurely
on his conquest
the innocent dead chest
of an immorally won trophy

DANGERS OF THE DEEP

Without emotion we humans
are polluting our oceans
slowly destroying
life sustaining
creatures of the sea

Poisonous remnants of war
plastic garbage galore
oil spills of greedy nations
and lethal doses of radiation
that the naked eye cannot see

It's not me telling you this
Pay attention to alarmed
oceanographers and scientists
who warn it's a problem
we cannot easily dismiss

Fish gotta swim—birds gotta fly
be extra careful of stuff you buy
Waste not want not is the solution
to stem the tide
of our human pollution

BIG AL

Al a big hairy ape
became tangled in tape
as he tried to escape from the zoo
No one came to his aid
'cause they all were afraid
of what Big Al might do
A Boy Scout in the crowd
shouted out loud
"Hey the same thing once
happened to me
If you just stay still
Scout's Honour I will
come on over and set you free"
Penknife in hand the scout cut each strand
releasing the ape from the tape
"It's a miracle" cried Al
to his new pen knife pal
and the crowd with their mouths all agape
Gratitude ensued from Big Al now subdued
yet without any loss of his pride
The scout with a cheer
said "Big Al's staying here
'cause he knows it's a jungle outside!"

MY FUNNY
FURRY VALENTINE

One of the best friends I ever knew
could only speak meow mew mew
Cleo was the most unusual cat
with whom I could sit and chat
To some it may seem absurd
but she understood my every word
A domestic tabby grey,
black and brown
who lifted my spirits
when I was feeling down
Her sweet nature silky fur
drooling kisses contented purr
Her beautiful eyes
soul searched mine
knowing when I was ecstatic
or tear soaked blind
At age nineteen she departed
leaving me bereft and broken hearted
No other creature in space and time
can replace my
funny, furry feline Valentine

FOR THE BIRDS

I do not twitter or tweet
that's for the birds
as they sweetly greet
an early dawn
searching for worms on
a dewdrop lawn

No dirty linen do they air
forcing strangers to stare
hearing vociferous voices
polluting the atmosphere

Birds don't bump, trip or fall
walking through a busy mall
distracted by a cel-phone call
and expletives that appal

Towers of Babble on the street
restaurants, airports and the beach
no respite from human screech
no escape and no retreat

Twilight descends birds depart
nesting refuge in soothing dark
renewing their sweet song
to herald a brand new morn

Cel-phone glued to you ear
a warning from me—stay clear
as I am tempted to shove the
damn device up your rear

HOLY COW

Beautiful big brown eyed cows
where do they go when
their milk no longer flows?

Their faithful service at an end
are our Creators gift abandoned
left to wander without a friend?

The cows of India are respectfully
revered with dignity and loyally
treated as sacred royalty

Our western cows do not share
the same rarefied stratosphere
as the revered cows of India

To the UK Dairy Industry
I proposed adorning old cows
with crowns and regal finery

Invite the Queen, Her Majesty
to endorse the Dairy Industry
proclaiming cow's milk a priority

Strengthening teeth and bone
cows are as essential
as she on her throne

Reaction exploded Winston style
my idea met with udder revile
accused of treason I faced a trial

I had provoked a national row
How dare I compare the Queen
to an old retired brown eyed cow?

But I stammered in self defence
to Her Majesty I meant no offence
cows are vital to human strength

In the witness box filled with dread
I was condemned the verdict read
'Show her no mercy off with her head'

'Any last words?' his Honour asked
'Yes I am innocent' I feebly gasped,
'no cream mo Royal Garden Party blast'

'The Queen's not an old cow' I lamented
The Judge his fury fermented
said 'Silence you are demented'

Expressing my idea as 'Holy Cow'
would have prevented
the mess I'm in now

Suddenly a sunlight beam
awakened me from my dairy dream
My head intact, no noos nor Queen

All serene, smooth as silk
awaiting me a bowl of Cheerio's
smothered in fresh milk

A HOLY COW EXPLANATION

Where the American epithet 'Holy Cow' came from is a mystery. Maybe it was derived from India, where cows are revered.

Affection for the animal species in our Western culture is focused on domesticated cats and dogs who embrace our snuggles and cuddles. Outside the domesticated realm adoration is showered on Pandas, Koalas and Llamas.

Treated with indifference are two of the most hardworking creatures on our planet, the 'Stupid Ass and 'How Now Brown Cow' My humorous cartoon book, Lyn's Ass Legacy, dispels disrespect for the Ass. Based on India's reverence for its cows has given me the impetus to elevate and dignify our beautiful, brown eyed docile bovines.

Unceasingly providing life's delicious sustenance, cow's milk strengthens teeth and bones. At any given moment our society enjoys milk and all of its properties; cream, butter, cheese and ice-cream. And who doesn't scream for ice-cream?

For these treasures alone our cows should be adorned with gold crowns and royal robes. Instead, they are ignored and demeaned with inane expressions, 'Not until the cows come home' or 'the cow jumped over the moon' and 'she's a cash cow'.

For centuries in my country, England an ugly, insulting epithet, 'A stupid old cow' is commonly used devastating the person to whom it is directed. It is however not without its comedic application and I hope the following anecdote pertaining to my feisty Aunt Ellen will bring a smile.

Gregarious redhead, brimming with humour and Music Hall songs Ellen was one of London's cherished barmaids. Employed at a prestigious Fleet Street pub she was adored by its clientele, famous barristers and reporters.

One year she was chosen to manage the Royal Bar during Ascot Week. Accompanied by two colleagues, Titch the handy man and associate barmaid, Daisy they arrived at Ascot at 4am and began preparations for the opening day.

Ellen busily polishing the mahogany bar was startled to see her Majesty Queen Elizabeth accompanied by an aide slowly walking towards her. Titch and Daisy unaware of the royal approach laughed when Ellen whispered, 'The Queen is here'.

Cockney Daisy responded to Ellen's whisper, "You stupid old cow 'er Majesty ain't up and abaht at this 'our'!" Annoyed, Ellen spun around retorting vociferously, "If I were a stupid old cow, I'd ram my ''orns up yer arse'.

Ellen's outburst was delivered at the precise moment when Queen Elizabeth the Second bellied up to the bar. With a smile, she graciously bid the three speechless subjects 'Good morning' and departed.

Known for her mimicry, the Queen in privacy may have delighted guests or threatened staff reiterating Ellen's colourful, 'Stupid old cow' comment.

I shall continue to convince the Dairy Industry to elevate the status of our precious cows—if not 'Holy 'how about a 'Bovine Beauty' contest?

Footnote: More fun stories about Ellen, my personal, 'Auntie Mame, are recorded in my autobiography, Brief Encounters.

CORRUPTION

**Ugly corruption surrounds us
everywhere
Unchallenged by those
who do not dare or care
Perpetrated by hedonistic greed
without remorse for those in need
Motive masked in thin disguise
Smoke., mirrors, deceptive lies
And when the truth is revealed
culprits demand their case repealed
The scales of justice are askew
The final verdict up to you**

CRIME

Solving a crime is a puzzle
Stabbed, beaten, smoking gun muzzle
It's up to the law to make pieces fit
ending the mystery of 'Who done it'
Those not involved unaware—don't care
unless you're a suspect in the
interrogation chair
Your alibi summarized
proving you've told no lies
The real culprit now in custody
freeing you to enjoy your liberty
The puzzle pieces fit together
finally the nightmare's over

FEDS AND FLIVVERS

The Wild Wild West
was never laid to rest
affecting generations to come
with an enticing message
it's okay to carry a gun
Lingering in the ancient shadow
Bonnie Parker and Clyde Barrow
Hero worshipped for
their outlaw criminality
until ambushed and
death set them free
Following prohibition
Hollywood influenced a nation
violence on its silver screen
iconic gangsters tough and mean
Mobsters and Molls claim to fame
Post Office portraits all unframed
fascinating the public's eye
ardently pursued by the FBI

Going to the Big House
and the Chair
not a five star hotel
in Palm Air
while law abiding
tax payers
paid their fare
Convicted criminals
in their steel barred cell
serving time on
which to dwell
next residence
heaven or hell?
Warning to those
engaged in violence
eventually you'll face
the consequence
Your freedom
will be curtailed
and the rest of your
life securely jailed

DEITY

There is no earthly deity
deserving of my piety
No human being
is so rare
commanding a
privileged stratosphere
Subjects pay homage
on bended knee
as icons ignore
their humble plea

Who gave permission
to Henry the Eight
to whacked off
wives heads
defiling a
religious debate?
This self indulgent
despot king
should himself felt
the axe man's sting

In sumptuous palaces
behind iron gates
awaits a life to which
we cannot relate
Diamond crowns
gilded coaches
Mesmerizing
Royal approaches
Pomp Circumstance
marching bands
Flags waving
in eager hands
Emblazoned uniforms
furs and feathers
saddled horses
brass and leathers

Remaining a mystery
in spite of
recorded history
who deemed this branch
of the human tree
the only earthly deity?

SPECIAL DELIVERY

If we all obeyed the
Ten Commandments
Imagine the affect of
our advancement
The scales of justice
balanced all the time
a nation void of any crime
An altruistic dream
I can hear the sceptics say
However I'll gently
remind you there
will come a day
when tears, fears and death no more
will be knocking at your front door
Then maybe you'll believe
in such a theory
An unexpected special delivery
free of charge no strings attached
welcome it with your heart unlatched
this precious package really exists
just one of Jehovah's precious gifts

EDWARD R. MURROW

'You Are There'
and
Where Are You?

We were never there
at the cross
to witness His body
dripping with blood
or climb aboard
Noah's Ark before
the flood
and watch
Moses parting
the Red Sea
the ultimate escape
to set his people free
Imagine the heavenly re-runs
shown tomorrow
by
You Are There
Edward R. Murrow

THE GREAT DRY
WALL OF CHINA

I deeply respect the Chinese
their food, culture and expertise
With their mass production
I'm ill at ease

Corporate America greedily
played the game exponentially
outsourcing surreptitiously
'Made in America'—past history

Consumer wolves in western woods
hungrily devoured cheap Chinese goods
Watching as their economy soared
we were the mouse that never roared

It took a while for us to realize
exotic toxins in Chinese merchandise
Proceed cautiously and be aware
read their labels with extreme care

Now a millstone round our neck
we owe China an enormous debt
Stop buying stuff you don't need
and stem the tide of corporate greed

ENIGMATIC NAPOLEON

who never let the left hand know
what the right hand was doing
proof—his famous quote
"Not tonight Josephine"
Was it a questionable plea or a command?
or a language misinterpretation
"Knot too tight Josephine?"
as he tied her dainty ankle to the bed post.

Then at the end of his rope
'Boney' the despotic dope
sat on his horse in the pouring rain
idling the rein aware his reign
was over
Banished to Elba—exiled forever
Her face wreathed in pain
Nap's mistress behind
curtained window pane
watched his departure
with distain
No more caviar or champagne
or to ever hear again
Expressed in reverie
"Knot too tight ma cherie?"

FADING FAST

My old blue jeans
are faded and torn
Feels I've worn 'em
since I was born

Memories sewn in
seams still exist
drunken nights,
my very first kiss

Rough tough fabric
taking its toll
drilling for oil
digging for coal

Time to part with
my old faded friend
covering my ass
and knee bends

Part we must
I've got a new job
suit, tie and a
pocket watch fob

No more roamin' around
at my own pace
Be on time with
clean shaven face

Sadly I'll bid
you adieu
maybe you'll
comfort somebody new

Faithful old blue jeans
faded and torn
Never forget
how well
we got along

DRUGGED

Drugs existed since
the beginning of time
Found in trees, plants and
primordial slime
Chewed, sniffed and
with a needle
creating chaos and
unstable people
Devious tunnels
underground
Coke and marijuana
USA bound
Billionaire cartels
thrive and kill
as you indulge in your
cursed thrill
Whether you are young
or in your prime
Stop your addiction
and end this crime

LEAVES

Golden leaves leave their trees
Gently fluttering into mounds
Crispy dry under an autumn sky
Crackling carpets covering grounds
Gleeful cries fill the air
as children toss the gold
without a care
announcing a season passing by
Bitter winds nip at nose and cheek
scarves and gloves appear
Silent flakes of glistening snow
coat land and timid deer
Our breath pours forth filmy white
floating on the frosty night
Inside secure and warm
avoiding the winter's storm
Melting ice softens the earth
emerging shoots arise
Balmy breezes caress the skin
heralding nature's prize
Naked trees are dressed again
embracing summer sun and rain
Canopies of cooling shade
until once more the leaves cascade

PAINFUL PAPER CHASE

Paper replaced by computers
the experts claimed
Today those pundits
shake their heads ashamed
My desk is piled sky high
with their myth a blatant lie
Advertisements and catalogues
selling useless crap
and I am caught in their web
of a painful paper trap
My name sold to an
unending mailing list
unheeded by threats of
legal action to desist
We must save our precious trees
Waving branches and cooling leaves
home to squirrels and twittering birds
their existence so far undisturbed
How long will it be before
they too disappear?
Satisfying unconscionable
human gear
an unlimited supply of paper goods
decimating forests and shaded woods
When the land is laid to waste
a wake up call a bitter taste

LOVE'S ILLUSION

Comets streak across the sky
in blue daylight and black night
catching you by surprise
in its brilliant mercurial flight

Love can catch you the same way
suspended in an euphoric mist
enveloped beyond time with his kiss
senses smothered in mystical spray

A city of lights, romantic nights
hearts flying higher than paper kites
whispered nothings in your ears
ending in copious tears

When it begins it is forever
when it's over no more together
Sorrow is sweet and so hollow
where do you go who do you follow?

Losing your place in the sun
your orbit has crashed and you run
wildly, blindly into the arms of another
hopefully this time it's your mother

Soothing your broken heart
words of wisdom she'll impart
Many romances are a delusion
be prepared for love's illusion

MARRIAGE

Marriage what a farce
they say it's
supposed to last
Your wedded bliss
and promised kiss
is now splitting apart
Honeymoon's over
He becomes a rover
slowly breaking your heart
The love you once knew
heaped on someone new
leaving you chagrined
alone in the dark
Next time make sure
your romantic allure
blows off steam like
Old Faithful in
Yellowstone Park

SNO JOB

I'd rather be wary of
Greeks bearing gifts
because I am weary
of geeks buried in
snowy drifts
If you're going to climb
mountains all alone
be like ET make sure
you call home
Contact the family
well in advance
in case you die
in an avalanche
Yes, I'd rather be wary
of a Greek bearing a gift
than swept away
in a blizzard
Get my drift?

THE MAN ON THE MOON

We shall never forget
your small footstep
embedded in the
dust of the moon
The Eagle Has Landed
you announced to the earth
thousands of miles
from your place of birth
Now you too have joined
the heavenly race
adventurous Neil Armstrong
exploring the infinity
of universal space

HOMAGE TO
A MAN OF HONOUR

His name is Ray
my landlord forever and a day
Goes beyond the call of duty
always the extra mile
with good humour
and a genuine smile
A dependable man
of integrity
taking great pride
with his property
No problem is
too small or great
Whether early or late
with the utmost care
he arrives to repair
my refuge and safe haven
my home, a slice
of earthly heaven
I pray Jehovah has in
His grand plan
a place of honour for Ray
a rare gem in the crown
of man

MARVELOUS MAYANS

What makes your blood boil
the price of oil
Wall Street's insatiable need
corruption and greed?
Or a mindless royal
on a toot in a suite
cocky and
nakedly indiscreet?
Is it the tax cut for the rich
and your car's in a ditch
or the check that never came
Then you lost your job
'cause your boss the slob
on you he put all the blame?
On top of all that
someone said you were fat
loose weight and go on a diet
More doom and gloom was said
as you prepare for bed
when TV news screamed
'Middle East Riot'
Stop worrying my friends
Mayan calendar portends
December 21, twenty-twelve
Planet Earth's nonsense shelved
and life as we know will end

OBAMA

Barak Hussein Obama
paid homage to
Mom and Grandmother
They taught him well
to speak and spell and behave
in a forthright manner
Encouraging his aspirations
unaware one day
he would lead a nation
On January 20, 2009
their talented child in his prime
sent thrills and chills
down everyone's spine
As Barak Hussein Obama
accepted graciously the responsibility
the 44th United States Presidency
Awarded the Nobel Prize
unconscionably criticized
by envious opponents who despise
dignified Obama erudite and wise
Thwarted at every turn
by a congress eager to spurn
Obama's efforts to reverse
mistakes made during Bush's term
A house divided cannot stand
Time to unite—extend your hand
Re-elect Obama, the 'Can do' man

ELECTION 2012

Joy to the World

How could this nation
so easily forget
Obama inherited
Bush's enormous debt?
His first four years were
spent untangling
the knots of
Republican wrangling
As his term neared
its end
re-election on
accomplishments
would depend
Opposition launched a
massive campaign
Full of promises and
feeble restrain
For months we
could not escape
television commercials
of presidential **candidates**

The battle began
a war of words ensued
frowns, smiles as
each one accused
dividing a nation
fifty-fifty
whether to be rich
or downright thrifty
I prayed to Jehovah
day and night
for Barak Obama
to win the fight
On November Six
he won four
more years to fix
after rhetoric subsided
a house divided
Joy to the World
The Lord be praised
for a leader
He had raised
to get this nation
back on track
Thank you Jehovah
Thank you Barak

POISONOUS POLITICS

He's a hunter and trapper
A devious dangerous player
controlling Washington soothsayers

Sponsors are corporate giants
with unlimited regard to finance
rewarding him with monetary radiance

A feared Washington lobbyist
forceful, manipulative and abusive
dismissing opponents as subversive

His pledges must be upheld
excuses and arguments quelled
or promising careers are shelved

Is he a racist, fascist or a nazi
controlling a major political party?
If so is this American Democracy?

SAME OLD GAME

If we had to start from scratch
what human condition would we hatch
on this planet of green and blue?
The final verdict is up to you
Thugs emerge from their cave
intimidating those less brave
armed with grunts and lethal stones
a legacy carnage of blood and bones
Weaving their barbaric thread
Opposition silenced sword to head
Tribal kingdoms rule the land
with iron fist in upper hand
Despotic dragons appear
spewing fiery hatred and fear
inflaming those unopposed
to enforce their illegal cause
A voracious appetite for war
evil plans even the score
between nations who disagree
proof on the pages of history
Empires fall into brittle rust
Coveted spoils return to dust
What lessons have we learned?
None I fear—all are spurned
Starting from scratch once again
who without shame is to blame
allowing barbaric thugs to claim
'We're playing the same old game'?

OVERLOADED

What triggers the brain
to unleash the pain
of an explosive murderous rage?
Mental disease isn't rare
it exists everywhere
as evidenced in every age

Our computer brains are complex
zillions of sound bytes and text
issued from intricate circuitry
racing through time and eternity
If a damaged wire gets switched
integrity and sanity gets ditched

Subconscious madness ferments
as roiling volcanic steam vents
with an explosive eruption
spewing death and destruction
with no conscious remorse
of the serious consequence

Solving the brain's mystery
answers of scientific accuracy
will be revealed to us eventually
Avoiding anger and urges to fight
instantly releases your soul
from darkness to light

SMART

Smart describes a stinging slap
or a
well dressed chap
and a
rebellious youth
whose language is uncouth
Smart can mean
you're bright and sharp
like soothing strings
of a harp
or a 'Smart Ass' epithet
uttered by
your boring boss
It's your gain and his loss
Accept this worn accolade
with a smile
you've earned it
by the dues you paid

A WIDENING GULF

You'll never catch me
eating shrimp from the sea
where BP spilled its guts
Offering slick oily excuses
I classify as nuts
Claiming a swift recovery
a carpet bagger's remedy
an elixir to cure your anxiety
Cleansing microbes of the deep
as wildlife and marshes struggle
to rest and sleep
A restoration Gulf Shore
promise BP can't keep

LIMERICKS

THE CURSE

Limericks are a disease and a curse
each word I utter a possible verse
repetitive thought in my brain
a melody I cannot restrain
this malady I fear will get worse

Analogous to Sherlock's Moriarty
my nemesis limerick stalks furtively
gleefully whispering in my ear
here's more words for you to hear
and transpose accordingly

Each line and meter must balance
discipline with flair and romance
no cure in sight for my addiction
no remission for this affliction
absurd verses of utter nonsense

Proving my point
the following you'll see
the absurd nemesis
haunting me

THE CLEVER PRAWN

An innocent prawn
mowing his lawn
under the deep blue sea
spied a hungry shark
hunting for afternoon tea
said smart prawn to the shark
come back after dark
my treat dinner's on me

A GRATEFUL SNAKE

A new skin I need moaned the snake
slithering alone near a dark lake
shut hp your rattle and be glad
you escaped from the charmer Bad
no longer do you have to dance
charming crowds into a trance
a big plus make no mistake
you're not on the menu
as grilled steak

POLAR BEAR

Whad'ya mean
a polar bear is mean?
Don't ya know
he's losing ice and snow?
His food supply is going fast
and he ain't gonna be
happy eating grass
The Navy Seals he don't like
'cause their rubber ain't blubber
and hard to bite
Start stacking up on all the ice
and be aware
our new neighbors maybe
the Polar Bear

TIGER

Tiger Tiger in the woods
doin' what other Tigers
wish they could
making lovely
nymphettes cry
as Tiger unzips
his Tiger fly

COMPROMISE

Politely we agree to disagree
civilized with no intermediary
our manner calm, dignified and poised
until your expletives explode with noise
and I punch you out for insulting me

OOPS

A newly wedded naïve bride
puffing up with wifely pride
made a huge mistake
when baking her first cake
she mixed in a flower instead of flour
giving hubby a debilitating stomach ache

TIME

To a child time is interminable
for ancient adults one day
from another becomes indiscernible
A blast from the past flashes fast
like the ice in your glass it won't last
While children anxiously count
each hour and day
anticipating jingle bells and Santa's sleigh

HOMONYMS

I do not shun the pun
yet relish the challenge
of having fun
with nun other than the
ubiquitous homonym

There are thousands of words
that sound the same and
yet have different meanings

example
A foul fowl with smelly feat
was shunned bye the hens he
was dyeing to meat

I urge you to try and you'll sea
ours of pleasure I guarantee
Sew reed on and bee come inspired
inform yore brain you haven't retired

And if you please
don't forget to dot your eyes
and cross your tease

Above Awl
mind your peas and queues

ALAS from ALASKA

Weighted at my iron gait
cursing the hour was getting late
drenched in freezing reign
for a taxi dermist who never came
My stiff and sullen mousse
yeah I cooked his goose
suddenly sprang to life
threatened me with a knife
Impaled me on the fence
bellowing 'Sarah you stupid wench
you really are of no consequence'
Me the guvner of Alaska
who can see the snowy steps of Russia
bullied by a bull nosed moose
who I shot as he ran loose
scaring us all before our supper
Me a vice president candidate
politics heaped up on my plate
ready to battle the Democrats I hate
hanging by a thread on my garden gate
McCain rescue me bee four its two late

SANTA PAUSE

Last Christmas Eve
home with the flu
Santa flew down
the flu with the flu
No stockings did he fill
poor chap he was two ill
pleading with hymn to stay
and forget about his loaded slay
with a sigh of relief
on the sofa he fell asleep
the rain dears anxious to go
even without Santa's Ho Ho Ho
jingled and jangled there belles
and took off like cricket
bats out of hell
sped up, up and aweigh
and like FedX
delivered the
goods in won day

SUCCOUR FOR SUCKERS

An ancient profit
maid a huge prophet
poking a whole in the
Mayan colander sprocket
His prediction red
count every heir
on your head
and you'll arrive at the number
of daze bee four yore dead

DRUNK AS A SKUNK

A gnu I new
vacationing in Peru
imbibed in two much brew
As he lay stinking drunk
observed by a skunk
who smilingly said
it's about thyme
for my smelly crime
yew can be blamed instead

WRITE TO BARE ARMS

defend your tattoos

SHORT STORIES

BEEF

An immensely popular television commercial featured a disgruntled, grey haired grandmother staring at a solitary hamburger and complains, 'Where's the beef?' I wondered if the creators of that commercial lived in Great Britain during World War Two where everyone asked the same question.

Beef, a word that immediately conjures up a childhood memory, the butcher's shop and its window of dangling sausages, unplucked fowl and sides of beef. When my mother could afford it she bought a succulent, beef roast. That meant her delicious roast potatoes, sweet peas from my father's garden, gravy and light as a feather, Yorkshire pudding was a treat to be relished.

On September 3, 1939 our little, sanguine family, Mummie, Daddie, my sister Irene and I sat at the oil cloth covered kitchen table for the last time to enjoy our Sunday roast beef dinner. We had all heard Neville Chamberlain's wavering voice over the wireless declare we were at war with Germany.

By 1940 all hell had broken loose, gasmasks, black out, air raids, sirens, threat of a Nazi invasion and for me, evacuation. My sister was conscripted to an ammunitions factory, my father an air raid warden. Scattered in the chaos; we were no longer a cohesive and secure family. The butcher's window was empty and food rationing was strictly enforced.

In retrospect the scarcity of pre-war food constituted a fairly healthy diet; fish from the dangerous North Sea, apples, plums and dark leafy vegetables. Gone were bananas, oranges and candy.

My mother queued for hours with other patient housewives willing to purchase whatever was available. Often at the end of the queue, a tired clerk mumbled, "Sorry Madame, we are all out!"

The Black Market thrived for those who could afford its exorbitant prices. My father adamantly opposed its existence accusing those involved as enemy collaborators. Defying our father, my sister purchased a pair of silk stockings from the forbidden source, a secret never disclosed.

A discreet population quietly contemplated if their Majesties were rationed. Everyone knew Winston Churchill still smoked his cigars and drank his vintage brandy.

One day I heard an American G.I. challenge another G.I. with, 'You gotta a beef?' My childish ears pricked up, what a delicious question; did the soldier have beef in his pocket? Endearing American expressions appeared to be connected to food when those brave soldiers called us 'Honey lambs and Curie Pies.'

A modern day immigrant to America at age nineteen in August, 1952, hot, tired and homesick I melted in the loving kindness of the Greenway family in Philadelphia. They were the in-laws of my best friend, Valerie. We two London lassies had married our G.I. Prince Charmings and began our American adventure together.

The gracious Greenway's insisted I was their houseguest while our husbands were discharged from their military service in nearby Ft. Dix. The

Greenway's magnanimous hospitality is detailed in my two autobiographies, Keep Your Pecker Up and Brief Encounters.

"Good morning girls," Mrs. Greenway announced as she did every morning, "Time for breakfast and today we are going shopping." I stood on the threshold of an emporium unlike any I had ever seen. Brightly lit, floors of sparkling white tiles, infinite aisles, shelves burgeoning with cans and packages; an Aladdin's cave, the America Super Market.

In front of the 'Fresh Meat' counter my glazed gaze tried to absorb the endless rows of beautifully packaged, veal, lamb, chicken and beef. Overwhelmed, the dam broke and I sobbed. Alarmed, Mrs. Greenway rushed to my side, "My dear, what's wrong?" As I tried to explain Valerie intervened, "Mom", she said, "Lyn feels guilty her family is still rationed and she isn't."

Unbelievably, in 1952 Germany and Japan recovered and prospered while Great Britain wallowed in drab austerity. Rationing was still in effect; a four inch piece of meat was considered a luxury as was one egg per person a week. In retrospect, my parents had fossilized from too much North Sea Fish and re-constituted eggs.

Stranded in their working class suburb with its small local shops they were unaware of Harrods's elegant, Food Hall and Fortnum & Mason shelves filled with coveted food products they could never afford.

Within a year, assimilating and pursuing the American Dream, I assuaged my guilt of residing in the land of plenty. My parents and sister received monthly care packages of canned fruit, chocolates, nylon stockings, soaps and tobacco, but no beef.

My large parcels were sent by sea, air mail was too expensive for me in the early 1950's. Fragile, fresh beef, would have never survived its two to three month sea voyage. By the time Omaha Steaks made its 'dry ice' debut my dear parents had passed away.

Today, there is no excuse for 'Where's the beef?" unless you are a vegetarian or a mad cow.

YOU GOTTA A BEEF?
You betcha.

Acclimating to American colloquiums I now understood the G.I.'s dissention, "You gotta a beef?" Joining the club of disgruntled 'beefers' I compiled my list.

Mouthing off won't cook the beef's goose, you have to take action. The action I took, 'Writing Wrongs' probably saved the United States Postal Service from bankruptcy.

The pen is mightier than the sword and wielding mine into powerful words of protests and compliments created a voluminous portfolio.

This wee small voice in the wilderness did achieve imperceptible results; a bus bench for the elderly, repair of dangerous railroad tracks and full blown media attention including their helicopters on an obviously slow newsday when I saved a drowning kitten.

I'll never give up penetrating the ivory towers of government and corporate America with solid proposals and solutions. To answer the little, grey haired lady asking, "Where's the bee?" here is the tip of my 'you betcha' iceberg.

My suggestions are simplistic. No need for bungling pundits espousing political rhetoric or dangling wrangling.

$AVE AMERICA

Benjamin Franklin's sage advice, "A penny Saved is a penny earned" is as easy as breathing. Adhering to Franklin's principle will put America back on its financial track.

$AVE AMERICA is a rewarding, risk free, savvy, secure savings plan designed to encourage every man-woman-child an opportunity to invest their money in the United States of America.

TAX FREE 5% INTEREST DIVIDEND
Minimum 2 Year Deposit $10 up to $150,000
FDIC insured.

NO COMPLICATED FINE PRINT LEGALESE

WARS

Get the hell out of tribal countries not interested in our idea of Democracy and withdraw ALL financial support

THE MILITARY

Deploy our military to win the drug war terrorizing our cities and borders. Corruptible nations who despise us and depend on our financial aid defend yourselves

THE MEDIA

Knock off the overwhelming coverage of self aggrandizement celebrities and icons. Focus on abused children, domestic abuse and feeding the hungry

DRUGS

Tax and legalize illegal drugs and free up our prisons for hardened criminals. We are capable of in-depth drug testing before issuing a driver's license

LIQUOR

Tax the same as cigarettes, caught DUI diver's license revoked permanency

OUTSOURCING

Incentive tax breaks for corporations not outsourcing manufacturing and services with proof Made in America

IMMIGRATION

This great country was forged by immigrants. Grant every alien a green card so they can work and pay their fair share of taxes allowing potential employer to hire without penalties. Agriculture needs the vital work force of the migrant worker.

Provide assistance to learn English, basic law, driving instructions before issuing a driver's license. The applicant will pay a reasonable fee to cover the costs of facilities and instructors.

BELIEVE IT OR NOT

No matter what your belief, just stop and feel the velvet petal of a rose, smell the sweet scent of a freshly moved lawn, breathe the air following a gentle rain.

In the wild or at the zoo you may have witnessed the voracity of a tiger, the antics of a chimpanzee, examined an ant farm, a honeycomb or viewed marvels through a microscope.

Depending on where you live a rose petal or a tiger may not be available. Some people have never seen the ocean. However, the expansive sky is visible to everyone.

Scientists inform us there are more galaxies than all the grains of sand on planet earth. In spite of space exploration no other planet has been found that compares to ours.

Earth is a speck of dust on the outer rim of the Milky Way. Photographed from the moon our unique planet appears as a blue green marble smothered in its life sustaining, balanced atmosphere.

The intricacies of the exceptional human brain are unfathomable. The genius of ancient civilizations paved the path toward our modern industrialization and space exploration.

The icing on the cake we are able to replicate ourselves through procreation, however, no human being has ever created a planet, a tree, or a flower.

Every second of every day and night the human race scurries or flies across the blue-green marble of mountainous beauty, rivers, fields, valleys, cities and oceans.

Diagnosing the human condition the majority of earth's population peacefully goes about its business while an unconscionable barbaric hedonistic 'element' spews religious venom, destruction and death.

The powerful 'element' has many agendas one of which has decent, concerned parents overwhelmed; a lethal drug epidemic enticing a generation unable to resist. Extricating their children from the scourge is hampered by bullying and the electronic web of internet.

You may ask where did it all begin? Drugs have existed since time immemorial. In the 1960's drug infused 'flower' children attending the Woodstock music festival created a movement and made headline news.

Protesting the Viet Nam war their altruistic message 'Make love not war' resulted in sexually transmitted diseases and abandoned children.

Adding to our human woes other cultures fiercely oppose a western lifestyle, self indulgence and religious beliefs. And again the question where and when did the fracture crack?

Ancient humans seeking refuge from the elements gravitated toward mystical entities to guard and guide them. Eventually their idolization developed diverse man made religious dogmas perpetrating intolerance and hatred.

The challenge of the 21st Century; convince a diverse religious global population to end superstition, intolerance and hatred. Why can't we adhere to a simple message, 'Be not judgemental and love your enemies?'

Analyzing my statements I am undeterred having overcome monumental barriers throughout my life. Maybe I am a cockeyed optimist but see a light at the end of a dark tunnel.

That light is my deep faith in Jehovah and His son, Jesus. I am not proselytizing only wanting to share important information. I urge everyone to read the Books of Daniel and Ezekiel in the Hebrew Scriptures that explicitly define 21st Century events especially the Middle East crisis.

Having studied all religions, I assure you my knowledge is based on unequivocal proof. Dozens of indisputable prophesies in the Old Testament were written hundreds of years before the birth of Jesus accurately detailing His name, lineage, life and death.

Following His resurrection over five hundred people witnessed His physical appearance including the Jewish historian, Josephus.

If just one person reading this epistle counts their blessings and gives thanks to our Creator for all the wonders on our spaceship paradise, I believe the message will be passed on. Ignorance is not bliss; am educated majority can defeat an unethical corruptive 'element'.

Whether you agree with me or not take time to appreciate the natural wonders surrounding you, love your family, friends, extend a helping hand to those in need, feel the velvety petal of a rose and think about its creator.

CHOMPING AT THE BIT

Snap Crackle & Pop
I envy the incredible shark
and his pearly whites
whenever he loses a set
another grows back overnight

Historically, due to poor nutrition, ignorance and fear the Brits have faced an unrelenting, international reputation for 'Bad Teeth'. Diametrically opposed, our American cousins obsess over their healthy, bright, white choppers aware a winning smile wins.

Adding insult to injury to the 'Bad Teeth' syndrome an overwhelmed British National Health Care system cannot cope with the population's demand for routine dental care resulting in a nation of denture wearers chomping on cheap plastic.

Thus begins my 'Chomping at the Bit saga.

In 1935 when I was three years old my mother crossed the palm of a gypsy with silver preventing me from becoming a member of the 'Bad Teeth Brigade'. My only sibling,, sister Irene nine years my senior remembered the gypsy encounter at our front door as I clung fearfully to my mother's skirt.

Our sweet, naive generous mother imbued with superstitious beliefs listened carefully to the gypsy's old wives tale ensuring good luck if my baby teeth were removed.

Superstition ran rampant in my mother's large family. Her aunts, sisters and female cousins delighted in reading tea leaves with promises of tall dark handsome suitors, travel and money which never materialized.

Gypsy superstitions were strictly observed; horse shoes for luck, toss salt over shoulders, touch wood, never walk under ladders, cover scissors during thunderstorms, cross fingers and avoid breaking mirrors.

Whisked off to the dentist, its terrifying experience is forever imbedded in my brain; the ether mask plunging me into unconsciousness, gagging and choking on coagulated blood in my throat.

The only 'luck' garnered from the ordeal, perfect teeth, strong, straight and white, ironically an inherited gene from my father. My mother and sister did not fare well in the 'chopper' department.

Superstition nonsense came to a screeching halt in September, 1939 when war with Germany was declared. Seeking solace my mother returned to her

Christian principles and carefully re-read the Holy Bible.

To her dismay she discovered her seemingly innocent participation in tea leaf predictions, omens and the occult was an anathema to our Creator and strictly prohibited.

Gypsies were always treated with respect and politely asked not to reveal any messages. The word 'luck' was removed from my mother's vocabulary and replaced with 'God bless'. Family teasing ceased when tea was rationed. Priorities were focused on the reality of survival.

Fast forward to the 1960's, my mother, sister Irene and husband Don chewed on cheap plastic dentures that snapped, crackled and popped with more frequency than a bowl of cereal.

On their first visit to America my beautiful sister Irene and handsome husband Don were the honoured guests at a dinner party given by friends of mine. Eloquent Don, a retired naval officer was asked to address the guests.

The first words out of his mouth were interrupted when his upper denture snapped in two. Deeply embarrassed, the poor guy retreated to the patio where our gracious hostess super glue in hand solved the problem temporarily.

The following summer we vacationed in France. Don was equipped with a new set of dentures. Dining at a chic French restaurant, Don's 'uppers' became embedded in a croissant and once again snapped in half.

Chastised by Irene for not bringing a spare pair the gallant Don removed the 'lowers' and we continued on our journey. Good humoured Don allowed us to call him the 'toothless wonder'.

Payback came a year later on our annual vacation in England's beautiful city of York. Eating a slice of pizza, Irene's face flushed as Don and I heard the familiar 'crack'. Dear, gallant Don did not chastise her for a missing 'spare pair'.

The hotel concierge said York had many dental labs that repaired dentures. Giving us general directions we set out on our mission. Strolling through the maze of York's twisting streets Irene and I were absorbed in the Georgian architecture.

We had stepped back into the 18th Century. Intriguing quaint wooden plaques hanging from exterior wrought iron brackets advertised businesses and services housed in the uniform two storey buildings.

Don appeared preoccupied when Irene pointed to a sign heralding a Dental Laboratory. Inside the front door a narrow staircase led us to the second floor and a smiling receptionist. Relieved when assured Irene's cuspids would be repaired by the next day we left.

The next morning, sunny and bright we prepared for a day of sightseeing starting at the famous York Railway Museum. Don suggested he leave us there while he retrieved Irene's teeth. Deciding to take the car we waved Don farewell and made a beeline for a coffee shop.

Arranging to meet Don on Platform Nine within the hour Irene and I sat patiently. Three hours passed with no sign of Don. Alarmed we were concerned he had met with an accident.

Approaching the Great Terminal Hall to seek help our seventy-six year old seafaring hero, bedraggled and distraught came into view. Guiding him to the nearest seat the exhausted, errant, errand boy smiled, held out Irene's teeth and said, "You'll never believe what happened."

Our laughing and crying startled other visitors as Don related his misadventure. After parking his car he became disoriented in the City of York. With no receipt or address from the lab he could not remember its location. Embarrassed he confessed he had not paid attention to our chatter about the quaint hanging signs, especially our designated dental lab.

Asking a stranger where the nearest dental lab was the answer; there were several located on various streets. The stranger pointed to a sign over Don's head and said, "There's one". Climbing the stairs he was greeted by a receptionist who upon checking her records exclaimed, "No sir we haven't your wife's teeth.'

Insisting she had, a polite exchange brought the manager to the front desk. He informed Don he had the wrong lab and that there were six other labs in the vicinity. By the third lab, there was no wind in our seafarer's sails.

The missing three hours were explained and on the fourth set of stair climbing Don claimed his reward. We embraced our brave tooth hunter with unbridled pampering. Cursing the cheap plastic choppers both swore never to leave home again without a spare pair.

At dinner that evening, the calm after the storm we laughed uncontrollably when I proposed the following that can only be described in verse;

A toothless Irene returns
to lab of wrong door
Tearful and pleading,
she would implore
"Where is my spouse
I sent the day before?
For hours I've been waiting
on Platform Nine
for that wayward husband of mine
I don't care if he's done a moonlight flit
I just want my teeth back so
once again I can chomp at the bit."

Of course we never consummated my fanciful prank and my 'Chomping at the Bit' story became a family favourite providing us with untold hours of merriment.

Now my two darlings are
in peaceful repose thus ending
their 'chopper' plight
with a reminder false teeth
are like stars
and only come out at night

THE FIRST AND LAST CHRISTMAS

Vivid memories are often imprinted in the brains of impressionable children. Mine began at age three. To this day the images, details and smells are still crystal clear and the experiences corroborated as absolute truth by family members.

Up until the age of six memories were unblemished, delicious and forged my character. Bathed in a large kitchen sink, the scent of Pears soap and talcum powder, an enchanting seaside cottage, a Pantomime with flying carpets, white rabbit fur muff and marching hat and the aroma of my father's pipe tobacco. The list is endless; however this story concentrates on my first recollection and experience of Christmas 1938.

My parents whom my sister Irene and I addressed as Mummie and Daddie were as poor as church mice. We lived in a modest flat on the top floor of 19 Canonbury Road, Islington, London, England. The only two children of our parents Irene and I were their treasures enveloped with love, affection and sweet discipline. Life was serene, secure, happy and uncomplicated.

My mother's only material possession was her second hand upright piano which she played beautifully. Untrained, unable to read a note of music she could play any tune by ear. To our utter delight she and Daddie who strummed his ukulele performed duets. Their music was derived from the Victorian and Edwardian 'Music Hall' era; lilting melodies and rollicking songs; music seldom heard today.

In early December of 1938 an excitement permeated our small flat. Mummie played tunes I had never heard before on her beloved piano. Her clear soprano voice sang of 'Hark the Herald Angels' and The First Noel. They were songs to welcome the baby Jesus on his birthday. When I asked if the stork was going to bring him the way he had brought me, my mother looked perplexed and then answered, "No".

A few streets from where we lived the famous Chapel Street Market bustled with activity. From the age of ten until she was about thirty years of age, the 'market' was my mother's Shangri La. Here on a meager budget she purchased groceries, fabrics, second hand shoes and an occasional trinket. Once in a while she indulged in a special teat at the Eel and Pie Shop.

A few days before my sixth birthday in December, 1938 I accompanied my lovely, gentle mother to her Aladdin's cave. Its narrow streets echoed with the coarse, jolly voices of vendors selling their wares from green canvas covered stalls.

Roasting chestnuts on red hot braziers wafted their delicious aroma on the cold December morning air. Pyramids of polished red apples, tangerines, oranges, fingers of bananas and plump black grapes greeted my eye level.

Staring up at a plethora of large lifeless feathered birds hanging by their webbed feet I quickly hid my face in my mother's coat. When I opened my eyes I was nose to beak with innocence deposited in my mother's large shopping basket.

The blue and white striped apron covering the front of the portly vendor was stained with blood. I was horrified. Pacifying my fear and tears my mother told me the goose was at peace and his feathers would make a soft pillow. The illusion was shattered when the vendor instructed my mother to 'Cook 'im slowly and save 'is fat'.

The bird was covered in white paper and hidden from view as we continued our shopping expedition. Stopping at the sweetshop I promptly forgot about forthcoming 'cooked goose' as a chocolate bar was placed in my hand followed by a visit to the chemist for a glass of Sarsaparilla.

Cheerful greetings were exchanged wherever we walked. It was obvious to me my mother was well known in her Garden of Eden. The hearty men and women behind the stalls called her 'Duckie' and asked, ''ows yer Mum luv?'

The next day our flat was in an uproar, sheets covered the parlour furniture, curtains were taken down and carpets rolled up. A strange man I had never seen before, wearing a black suit and cap carrying long brooms arrived and I learned he was the chimney sweep. Finished with his work he winked at my mother and said, "All's clear for Father Christmas."

Who was Father Christmas I wanted to know? Spellbound I listened as my mother described a round, jolly man in a red suit who lived at the North Pole with hundreds of his elves busy making toys. Once a year at night, he traveled the whole world in his sleigh pulled by dozens of reindeers who landed on roofs while Father Christmas popped down clean chimneys of good little girls and boys and left them a toy.

It was an impossible concept for my childish brain to comprehend. All I knew of the world was India and its staving children and that I must be grateful for the food on my plate and to eat all my vegetables. Asking my fourteen year old sister Irene if this jolly man had landed on our roof and come down our chimney she assured me he had and where did I think my Golliwog and china doll came from?

Showing me her painting set and roller skates she said Father Christmas had brought the year before. After the chimney sweep left my mother became a whirlwind; curtains were washed, re-hung, floors scrubbed, and the smell of wax polish mingled with wisps of smoke from Daddie's pipe tobacco.

In our small kitchen delicious aromas emanated from the gas stove oven. Wiping her hands on her apron Mummie cheerfully declared, "My darlings we are all ready for Father Christmas who arrives tonight."

Ritualistically every evening at seven o'clock, Irene and I were bathed, sprinkled with talcum powder put on nightdresses and prepared for bed. I wanted to stay up and see Father Christmas. No one was allowed to see him Daddie explained because he was 'too busy'; a remark I heard often in my life!

We said our prayers and Irene asked our Heavenly Father to make sure Father Christmas came down our chimney adding "Let's listen for his reindeer hooves." As we lay in the darkened room the only sounds I heard were muffled voices of Mummie and Daddie laughing and talking that soon lulled me to sleep.

Dawn's early light filtered through our bedroom window. The door flew open and Daddie cheerfully announced, "Get up sleepy heads, come and see what Father Christmas has brought you." We scrambled into our slippers and dressing gowns and entered the parlour. Overnight it had been transformed into a glistening fairyland.

Transfixed, I tried to absorb the glittering scene. Garlands of holly draped over the mantelpiece and picture frames twinkling with silver strands of tinsel. Bunches of Mistletoe hung from doorways, colourful paper chains and bells were strung across the parlour ceiling.

My attention was riveted on a tall green tree unlike any I had ever seen. Attached on its prickly branches tiny candles flickered and twinkled surrounded by silver tinsel garlands and glass icicles.

"Did you hear the reindeer's hooves and jingle bells on the roof last night?"` Daddie said with a wry smile. "No, Daddie," Irene and I answered together. "He was here," Daddie continued, "look at the mantelpiece and you'll see he filled your stockings hanging there."

Overwhelmed I did not know where to look first. Suddenly by the piano I noticed another object I had never seen before, a huge brown and white rocking horse with a long tail. Daddie hoisted me up into the saddle, said "Hold on tight" pulled down on the horse's nose and I rapidly rocked. It was the most thrilling ride I had ever encountered.

Irene cried out loud, "Oh, oh look what Father Christmas brought me, a typewriter!" Climbing off my magical horse I went to her side to inspect her new treasure. Mummie said "There are so many other presents waiting for you both." I was led to an exquisite two storey dolls house with windows, doors, fireplace and a staircase. Miniature furniture filled every room illuminated by tiny light bulbs.

On a well oiled hinge, the front of the house swung open smoothly revealing a fascinating interior. In awe, Irene and I fingered the tiny chairs and tables. Next to the fairytale residence two small china dolls lay on pink silk pillows covered by a pink silk eiderdown in a wooden rocking crib. My mind reeled with excitement.

Later I learned the masterpieces; doll's house and crib were crafted from my father's rough hands. My mother was an expert seamstress who did not own a sewing machine. Her nimble fingers stitched every item of clothing that Irene and I wore. Not a scrap of fabric was wasted and transformed into a wardrobe for our dolls.

Hot cocoa and 'Digestive' biscuits were served as Irene and I sat cross legged on the rug in front of the fireplace emanating warmth from its grate heaped with brightly burning coal. Two large, bulging red felt stockings were removed from the mantelpiece and plopped into our laps.

Our eager hands reached inside and pulled out a myriad of treasures; chocolate coins wrapped in gold foil and mesh, a miniature tea service, a matchbox that opened into a completely furnished room.

Irene's stocking contained grown up items; a fountain pen, a necklace, a pretty scarf and shiny ornaments for her hair. Each of us found tissue paper hats, whistles, a tangerine, a shiny silver sixpence and a lump of black coal. Mummie explained the coal was for 'luck'. Daddie snuffed out the candles on the tree and said it was time to get dressed for our weekly walk to London.

How well I remember our glorious weekly tours of London. Holding Daddie's hand as he described our history; looking through the iron gates of Buckingham Palace, staring up at Big Ben and the House of Parliament. We always rode home upstairs on a red double-decker bus. Irene and I sat up front looking at our city from wide windows while Daddie contentedly smoked his pipe.

In matching coats with velvet collars, white rabbit fur hats and muffs Irene and I waved goodbye to Mummie who reminded us to be home by five o'clock for our special Christmas dinner. Daddie said we were taking the underground today because time was running short. The lift doors clanged shut and we slowly descended into the bowels of the earth.

To this day I love the smell of the deep earth emanating from London's efficient underground railway system. On the platform I peered into the black tunnel and watched the approaching gleam of a headlight. It was our red train ready to carry us to Piccadilly Circus. Again for the first time I would see decorated shop windows as glittering as our parlour.

Promptly at five o'clock we arrived home and as we climbed three flights of stairs to our flat our nostrils were filled with delicious aromas. The kitchen table had been moved into the parlour and looked bigger. Covered in starched white damask crisply rolled linen napkins and decorated with the ubiquitous 'Bon Bon Christmas cracker'

'Crackers' were eight inch rolled tubes of cardboard wrapped in colourful tissue paper, embellished with gold and silver medallions. At each end the tissue was pinched and fluted. Inside the tube a strip of sulfurized paper issued a loud crack when pulled apart and out tumbled a myriad of delightful surprises; mementoes, whistles, puzzles and incredibly tiny folded squares of tissue paper that blossomed into crowns and party hats.

We sat down and gave thanks to our Heavenly Father for what we were about to receive. Then Mummie and Daddie disappeared and returned with Daddie carrying a huge plate on which sat the plump, golden goose. Although I never ate goose again, it was cooked to perfection along with Mummie's delicious roast potatoes, Yorkshire pudding and gravy.

Satiated, we laughed and chatted. Daddie once again disappeared. Mummie sat at her piano and with gusto played a rousing overture. Daddie reappeared this time with a large, half rounded black object enveloped in blue flames. Just as he had snuffed out the Christmas tree candles, to my relief he quelled the blue, flickering flames and I was introduced to the 'Christmas Pudding'.

Never had I tasted anything so delicious. Smothered in fresh cream I slowly savoured my mother's piece de resistance. I was warned to chew carefully in case I found one of the silver thrupenny bits buried in the mixture. Suddenly I remembered my mother preparing her puddings. It was on a lovely summer afternoon. She and Daddie stood at the kitchen table taking turns to stir black currants, eggs, milk and flour in a huge chima bowl.

As Mummie dropped silver coins, Daddie poured beer and rum into the mixture which was then transferred to four smaller bowls, topped with wax and wrapped tightly in white muslin. The bowls were placed in a large pan of steaming water on top of the gas stove. Hours later they were removed and sat on the window sill to cool. The next day the bowls were wrapped in brown paper put on the marble larder's shelf as Mummie said, "That's where the little dears will stay until Christmas."

As dusk drew into night I sat on Irene's lap as Mummie played the piano and Daddie prepared tea. He set the table with cups and saucers and plates of sandwiches. Once again Daddie disappeared and return bearing a large round cake covered in white icing and pink rosettes. On top was a sprig of holly and Mummie's handwriting in red icing that said, 'Merry Christmas'. It was the most magical time I could ever remember.

In the early summer of 1939 I watched intently as my mother prepared her 'little dears' for the marble larder shelf. This time I was allowed to drop silver sixpences into the mixture. This time I knew who Father Christmas was and that the world was much larger than I had imagined. I also became acquainted with the wireless in our kitchen where I listened to 'Children's Hour'.

On September 3rd I heard the wavering voice of Prime Minister Chamberlain declare we were at war with Germany. War and Germany were two words I had never heard before or understood.

The expression of fear on my parent's faces told me something dreadful was about to happen. Without warning within a few weeks I was whisked away from my beloved parents and sister to an unknown destination and into the arms of abusive strangers.

At age seven I learned Father Christmas was a fictitious character. I never again experienced those halcyon uncomplicated days of family unity. We were bombed out twice, losing everything, my rocking horse and dolls house smashed to smithereens. The magic of early childhood disappeared and I had to grow up fast.

Along with thousands of war weary children and their parents recapturing that pre-war era was impossible. Post war Britain was austere, drab and faced a deep depression. Subsequent Christmases were not celebrated in our humble abode. My father was too ill and my mother struggled to maintain a semblance of stability and cheerful optimism.

Both my beloved parents and sister have gone home to be with Jesus. I personally celebrate His existence every day and night without tinsel, carols and jingle bells. However, I do thank Him for that one precious memory of a dazzling childhood fairy tale lovingly created by my parents, Emily and George.

THE GRANDEUR OF OPERA

'It ain't over 'til the fat lady sings'—an ignoramus comment mocking opera. A negative message discouraging the uneducated from experiencing the incomparable music of genius composers, magnificently sung by trained human voices.

Few have any idea of the dedication, discipline and rigorous vocal calisthenics imperative to sustain the intricate purity of singing the soaring arias of Puccini, Verdi, Massenet, Wagner and Mozart.

If they were alive today, Rogers, Hammerstein, Cole Porter, Jerome Kern, Gershwin, would severely chastise those for neglecting the grandeur of the maestros from whom we derive our modern music. Proof; a pop culture, pathetic, tuneless, nasal, whining contestants vying for their fifteen minutes of fame on television.

Except for the sweet voices of the Children's Choir ringing out Elgar's 'Jerusalem' the 'music', or forgive me, the 'noise' chosen to represent Great Britain during the opening and closing ceremonies of the 2012 Olympic Games was a disgrace. I was ashamed of being a Brit.

The mindless producer, Danny Boyle made my blood boil. He must be deaf, certainly dumb and blind heaping rubbish on our green and pleasant land. The image he portrayed to the world; raucous rock, screeching guitars, thrashing drums, accompanying unintelligible, frenzied performers, an abysmal and an unconscionable production.

Not a note, not a scintilla of Britain's glorious, historical, melodious musical repertoire was heard in that vast stadium. Not a vestige of Benjamin Britten,, the joys of Victorian and Edwardian Music Hall, Ivor Novello, Noel Coward,, Julie Andrews, Andrew Lloyd Weber and our own grand Covent Garden Opera.

At age fifteen I attended the 1948 Olympiad held at Wembley Stadium. The atmosphere was charged with electricity and we were enveloped in victorious dignity. Heralding silver trumpets triumphantly rang out crystal clear announcing the monumental opening and closing ceremonies. That summer of 1948 was the most thrilling experience of my young life.

British teenagers had not been influenced by their screaming, writhing American counterparts dying for a glimpse of crooner, Frank Sinatra. Two generations would pass before the British 'screaming gene' kicked in with the advent of the Beatles.

Fuelled by television, the rebellious 'Mod' syndrome swept the country. Twiggy, who lived a few streets from me, was their poster child. Yes, I wore short skirts, Vidal Sassoon hairstyles and became dismayed with changing speech patterns. The rebellion had begun.

Britain's despicable class system died during World War Two and reared its ugly head the moment peace was declared. Although classified as working class I was taught to speak beautifully and suffered its consequences. Undeterred, I continued to pronounce clearly and distinctly and became an opinionated speech snob.

Upper crusty had been replaced with downright murky. Avoiding peer pressure the Mod Squad resorted to 'demotic argot.' the slovenly, lazy language of ordinary folk unwilling to invest in diction and dulcet tones.

Vowels, consonants were swallowed, chewed and gulped. Every dialect sprouted slang and the ubiquitous hey, hey, yeah yeah, ooh, ooh baby. Voices were mangled garbled and as irritating as their so called 'music'. Melodious was nowhere to be found in the Mod vocabulary

Poor as church mice, my beloved parents made sure at an early age I was introduced to music. It began with the piano that my mother played, the Music hall and its lively, melodious songs my father loved, the Albert Hall, Sadler Wells Ballet and grand Opera at Covent Garden.

The eclectic musical journey that has enriched my life continued with Britain's Ivor Novello's, musical productions, America's Rogers and Hammerstein, Leonard Bernstein, the magic of 'Broadway', Lincoln Center and classical jazz.

I am indebted to the 'Fat Lady' wearing a Viking horned helmet belting out Wagner from her ample bosom and the patrons who continue to support the grandeur of Grand Opera electrifying and delighting non-ignoramuses.

HANDS

Sobbing I cried out to my Aunt Ellen, "I want my Mummie". Fun loving, childless Aunt Ellen had whisked me off for a weekend at her lovely seaside bungalow, probably to give my mother a break. Never separated from my mother before I missed her beautiful face, calm voice and comforting hands, I was three years old.

Her hands were rough from scrubbing doorsteps when she was heavily pregnant with me. Her lovely face, peaches and cream complexion and huge brown eyes exuding love was all I knew.

Her right hand held my small left hand as we approached a large red brick building behind black iron gates. Its forbidding long corridor smelled of wax polish and disinfectant. I was terrified by the strange surroundings.

From nowhere a giant lady stood before us. As my mother ushered me toward the giant I cried out, "I hate you Mummie." A slight tap on my wrist and a verbal reprimand my mother warned I was to obey the giant, and abruptly left. The giant led me to a room dominated by a huge dolls house in which a dozen other children romped. It was our first day at infant school. I was four years old.

My father's calloused hand held mine as we stood in a restless group of grownups and children at Islington Town Hall. Long trestle tables heaped with black objects crowded the columned corridors. A new smell assailed my nostrils, the pungent odour of rubber. The black projects were gasmasks; World War Two had been declared.

The next day armed with my gasmask, linen knapsack and a label pinned to the velvet collar of my coat I reluctantly let go of my mother's hand as I boarded a bus to an unknown destination. I was six years old.

My nose pressed against the glass window of the bus as I watched my mother's tearful face and her fluttering hands touch her mouth blowing kisses. Several months would pass before I felt her hands again rescuing me from abusive strangers designated as care givers.

Diagnosed with throat cancer my father bravely faced a six hour laryngectomy operation. In the recovery room, I held his limp hand as he slowly opened his sad eyes. The strength of his hands with which he had hoisted me on his shoulders as a child, was gone.

As my father slowly recovered, I helped him tend his beloved garden. His breathing laboured he could only putter. He was forced to retire on a small pension and I became the breadwinner. I was fourteen years old.

Having potted plants, digging in garden dirt, scrubbing and cleaning, a myriad of lotions and manicurists kept my hands silky and smooth. Guilt ridden with my pampering luxuries, I tried gifting my mother with beauty salon expeditions which she adamantly refused. Guilt was assuaged when my parents accepted my financial support.

As my dear parents fossilized they were proud of their rough skin proving a life of humble hard work. Embracing each other for the last time on separate occasions the feel and touch of those strong, honest calloused hands are forever etched in my memory bank grateful for their guidance and love.

IMAGINE

London, September 1939 at age six hurriedly separated from my beloved parents I was on a train to an unknown destination and into the hands of abusive strangers. I survived—those to follow did not.

You are eighteen attending the University of Berlin. In the afternoon you will be crammed into a cattle car with hundreds of strangers. You will never see your parents again.

1943 in the Deep South you are a Black American, a welder in a Mobile, Alabama shipyard. Vicious white co-workers unleash their racist violence.

In your thatched Somalia hut preparing the evening meal you hear gun shots, flames and blinding thick smoke prevent your escape.

Breathing the rarefied air of the Himalayas, spinning prayer wheels you encounter a Chinese soldier who strikes your head with his rifle and shoots.

Disobeying your father in Bangladesh he cuts off your nose and ears—you die from infection.

Swiftly ascending to your 80th floor office at the World Trade Center on September 11, 2001 cheerful morning greetings are silenced.

Millions of words and images are proof positive evidence of the atrocities imposed on millions of human beings who suffered and perished satisfying the thirst of murderous unconscionable despots.

1945 at the cinema newsreel footage of the Holocaust horror caused my father to stand up and vehemently address a startled audience with seven words forever embedded in my brain, 'Mark my words it will happen again!'

Today my father's words ring loud and clear. Even with proof positive of Berlin, Alabama, Somalia, Tibet, Bangladesh and 9/11 the barbaric cycle continues. Apathy is not justice, silence is not golden, we must keep vigil and speak up whenever inalienable rights are violated.

IMAGINE you are an elephant and NEVER FORGET!

THE MUSIC LESSON

I have written in depth about my beautiful, lovely sister Irene in Keep Your Pecker Up and Brief Encounters and to whom this book is dedicated. What I omitted from her literary portrait was her fascination with music.

She loved to tap dance to syncopated tunes. Given dance and acrobatic lessons she was offered a major role in a 'Pantomime'. Our beloved Daddie refused to let Irene pursue a theatrical career because he was afraid of thespian degenerates who might influence her.

Secretly our Mummie allowed her to continue with dancing lessons. When I was six years of age and Irene was fourteen, I clearly remember her red tap shoes with floppy red bows rat tat tatting on the linoleum floor.

During heavy air raids she tried to divert our fear with a performance on the mosaic tiles of our long apartment corridor. Once a week in spite of heavy air raids she and her girl friends attended London's popular ballroom, the Hammersmith

'Palais de Dance'. Here they glided across the highly polished floor in the arms of American G.I.'s to the big band sound of Jimmy Dorsey and Glen Miller.

Irene loved and knew all the latest American songs; 'Tangerine, I'll Be Seeing You, Sentimental Journey and the Andrew Sisters, Bugle Boy Boogie'. She learned to jitterbug and tango. Blonde and beautiful she attracted many dance partners with absolutely no 'hanky panky'. A tall, dark and handsome American paratrooper captured her heart and was killed in the Battle of the Bulge.

Recovering from her loss, she fell in love with a dashing British Naval officer, Donald Edgecombe Rolph. They married and lived in Bermuda for a year. Returning to England they settled down to a country lifestyle in Don's ancestral home in Cambridgeshire and produced three children.

Our family changed drastically, I married and immigrated to the United States. Annually I spent my summer vacations with my beloved family in England where peace and pleasure flowed like wine.

One summer afternoon a young man appeared at Irene's kitchen door. He was extremely shy and his faced flushed red when we were introduced. His name was Simon and he was Irene's piano teacher. I almost fell off the kitchen chair 'Piano lessons!' "Yes", Irene said proudly, "you are not the only one in this family with musical talent!"

Had she forgotten? Both our parents were extremely musical. Our mother played the piano beautifully by ear and our father strummed a ukulele. In fact my mother's side of the family were musically inclined.

Before the war when we gathered at Auntie Hettie's home for her marvellous parties everyone, children and adults were expected to perform a 'party piece'. Her parlour reverberated with music and laughter.

Those parties remained forever in my memory bank. My mother's piano accompaniment to her sister Ellen's rich voice belting out favourite 'Music Hall' songs, my father imitating Britain's famous entertainer, George Formby `and his ukulele and Irene tap dancing on the highly polished floor.

My sister's jibe referred to my extensive knowledge of classical music and Broadway musicals. Adding insult to injury she disappeared into the lounge and returned with an album. The cover featured a picture of man's face encased in a white mask and the title "Phantom of the Opera'

"Ever heard of this?" she said defiantly. "No" I replied. "Well then" she continued, "you Yanks don't know everything, do you?" Andrew Lloyd Webber my dear is just as famous as your Rogers and Hammerstein."

Irene and I jousted often, we loved teasing each other. She was nine years my senior and when I was ten I became her nemesis, nicknamed the 'Little horror'. At each stage of my development Irene added new nicknames; Ninky Poo from my role as 'Nanky Poo in the Mikado and finally 'Lady Jane Grey' that described my pursuit of glamour.

I retaliated, calling her my personal 'Mrs. Malaprop' the delightful, comical character in Sheridan's 'The Rivals'. Although it was never discussed Irene may have been dyslectic as she innocently mangled certain words that left us laughing hysterically. I regret not writing them down but two I clearly remember are; elections were erections and flamingos were flambingos.

Patient Simon shuffled and slowly sipped his cup of tea as Irene turned on the hi-fi and played the Phantom recording. I listened intently to one of the most beautiful musical scores I had ever heard. 'Phantom' had not made its Broadway debut and I was ignorant of its existence. Jousting over it was time for Irene's lesson.

When I immigrated to America I had given Irene my lovely upright piano thinking her children would enjoy the instrument. Sadly none of them showed any interest. Simon sat next to Irene on the piano bench and placed a sheet of music on the rack. I was impressed, my fun loving, comical, delightful sister could read music and I could not.

Irene was left handed and fumbled as her fingers tried to coordinate the keys on a piano badly out of tune, it was abysmal. Stick to tap dancing I said silently. After a half hour of misplaced notes I smiled sweetly at Simon who gently chastised Irene for not practising.

I had inherited my mother's gift for playing the piano by ear. My living room possessed a sleek concert grand piano that I kept tuned to perfection. On her many visits to America Irene would ask me to play her favourite melody, 'Laura's Theme' from Dr. Zhivago.

Whenever I hear that soul wrenching theme I weep and yet smile with joy remembering my beautiful Irene and her lovely husband Don, my supreme audience and our wonderful times together in England and in America.

The last time I played 'Laura's Theme' for Irene was in September, 2001 on her piano, still badly out of tune. We never saw each other again. I could no longer fly due to deep vein thrombosis and my darling Irene was confined to her environs due to a severe heart condition.

We spoke on the telephone almost daily. In January, 2007 Irene was diagnosed with incurable bone cancer at the same time I was diagnosed with breast cancer. I underwent a double mastectomy and chemotherapy. Never had I felt so helpless as my beloved Irene sank, no longer able to speak or hear. On the last day of my radiation in October of 2007, my beautiful brother-in-law, Don called, Mrs Malaprop had gone.

All I hope and pray for is one day we shall be together again to love, verbally joust, laugh and I can play 'Laura's Theme' for the fumbling fingered music student with smiling hazel eyes, the dearest loving soul who ever existed.

MYSTERIES

Advanced ancient cultures, Egyptian and Mayan pyramids, quantum physics, an infinite cosmos are just a few of the deepening, unanswerable mysteries plaguing humankind.

Superseding an expanding universe, stone carvings and parchment documents found in caves cannot compare to an inexplicable mystery that continues to haunt me; a simple four letter word, love. A subject no one can clearly define. Is it chemical, animal, vegetable or mineral?

A potent, poetic quotation, 'It is better to have loved than not at all' played havoc with my blossoming feminine psyche. Impersonating Anna Karenna's unrequited affairs and a fairy tale Cinderella promise of 'Happy Ever After' a plethora of Prince Charmings on their snow-white steeds thundered in and out of my forest.

Pandora's Box was opened. Romantic flowers and flattery disguised and diffused quivering lust as cocky suitors sniffed, crowed, preened and pounced. Sexual passion ruled the roost;

two bodies entangled in each other's nakedness, drowning in orgiastic ecstasy.

Diagnosing a myriad of mysterious symptoms; puppy love, infatuation, fatal attraction as a persistent itch that had to be scratched I began my search to cure this annoying condition.

Burning the midnight oil and many martinis I discovered a rare mathematical combination to the safe in my heart. It didn't stop the itching but gave me a clue how to handle a lasting love investment. Two equals one if enveloped in the safety of euphoric, mutual warmth.

Band-Aids removed, my theoretical equation was ready to be tested. Out of the blue a soothing balm arrived on my doorstep. He was the antithesis of all the grandiose, Prince Charmings professing quasi 'happy ever after' promises.

The antithesis proved my theory, two equals one as he wrapped me in his secure blanket of euphoric warmth I believed was genuine love.

At thirty-eight years of age, I was a ripe Polly Anna melon who thought I had died and gone to heaven. I didn't heed the screaming alarm in my heart safe. The antithesis was a green restless cucumber.

I am ashamed to admit my theory fell apart as I did. The heat dissipated, the flame sputtered leaving a lingering scent of after shave lotion embedded in his bathrobe and a lonely pillow.

Now one, my wounded heart slowly healed and I continued my journey sidestepping trails of memories stopping occasionally to rest at pleasant nostalgia.

Who are we mysterious, flowering, mercurial, animalistic beings creating passionate alchemy with each other? Easing the windmills of my mind I anticipate answers to all mysteries will be revealed by the Creator of all mysteries.

At the edge of mortality, I fervently pray my future existence is wrapped in euphoric enveloping warmth with cherished family, friends and pets in the harmonious promise of eternity without a scintilla of rust, dust and Prince Charmings.

ORANGE

A sweet short story

Unleashing its deadly cargo, the Luftwaffe pounded London as my mother and I hurriedly left the safety of the Underground to board a Bristol bound train at Paddington station.

Dimly lit platforms teemed with anxious departing and arriving passengers greeted by shrieking whistles, hissing steam and impatient porters.

Inside a dust streaked cream coloured carriage crowded with restless American G.I.'s and choking cigarette smoke, a seat was offered to my mother.

Sitting on her lap, we both trembled with fear. There was no escape from the unrelenting bombarding terror surrounding us. Slowly the train edged its way out of the terminal, halted and stopped.

"Jeez" an American soldier declared, "we're gonna get it right here, right now!"

His ominous words were silenced by loud cheers as the train suddenly jerked forward and gathered speed.

"He's gonna make a run for it," another G.I. called out adding, "open the window Buddy and let's get some fresh air in here".

The city's night sky flared bright red as sweeping white searchlights caught trails of bursting blue, green flashes from our defending anti-aircraft guns. I had experienced countless air raids but never on a moving train.

Racing through the suburbs and across open country the horrendous explosions diminished. A sigh of relief swept through the carriage easing the tension.

A G.I. offered my mother a cigarette which she gratefully accepted. Her face was pale in the lighter's flame and her left arm held me tightly.

Another GI stood up and reached for his duffle bag sitting on the string luggage rack above his seat and with a heavy thud the bag rested by his booted feet.

Addressing me he said with a slow drawl, "Hey, young lady I betcha you'd like an orange, huh?" Surprised and startled I eagerly replied, "Yes please."

Smiling, he announced, "I hail from Florida, the 'Sunshine State' the land of oranges." and handed me a golden treasure, my first orange since 1939.

Delicately removing the outer skin of the precious fruit I broke apart each section delighting in its sticky residue. Offering to share my treasure with everyone I was politely refused and told to enjoy every thirst quenching morsel.

Roaring with laughter, the American G.I.'s said I was 'cute' when I vowed never to wash my hands again so I could always smell 'orange'.

On leave from frontlines fighting for our freedom the American soldiers in that smoke filled carriage disguised their exhaustion with easy going camaraderie and laughter. My mother and I never forgot that train ride and the privilege of being in the presence of real live American heroes.

The generous G.I. who hailed from Florida had no idea the precious orange was a symbol of my future; round, juicy, annoying 'pit' falls, pithy, bitter, delectable and golden.

At ten years of age on that 1942 train ride, I had no knowledge of Florida. In 1952 at age nineteen I immigrated to the United States of America residing in Minneapolis, Minnesota for sixteen years and in 1968 I moved to Manhattan, New York.

I have visited almost every state gracing this great land interspersed with trips to Europe, Bermuda, Mexico and the Caribbean. Never in my wildest dreams would I come home to roost 'golden years' in the Sunshine State with its Orange logo, my slice of earthly paradise for the past forty-one years.

A wartime orange represented days and years of my existence; a joyous, juicy journey bursting with exuberance, sticky situations dotted with intermittent distractions dissipating with fascinating, fragrant friendships.

Often I think of that special G.I. who hailed from Florida, wondering what became of his life and if anyone ever handed him a treasure.

THE SUNSHINE STATE

A continuum of my 'Orange' story is about the state of Florida and a man called Michael Scully.

A resident of Florida for over forty one years, I have traveled up and down the east and west coast, swum in the Atlantic, never in the Gulf, been to all of its major cities by car and plane and never realized its interior beauty until January 11, 2013.

Seated a height above a car on a Greyhound bus driven by an exceptional man, Michael Scully I enjoyed his knowledge and colourful history of our unique state as we crossed from East to Wes.

Although I am legally blind I can distinguish geography and experienced the wild, untamed Florida I had never seen before. A vast undeveloped land, patches of dense woodland reminiscent of Bavaria's Black Forest, beige bleached Everglades, an unending horizon of rich, black soil of sugar cane country.

An immense blue sky unfolded with dreamy white clouds that appeared as fluffy kittens extending their paws. Amusingly and as casually as any tourist, lazy Alligators with mouths wide open sunned themselves on the side of the highway. For miles not a human being or vehicle was visible.

My inquisitive mind had led me to a career as a writer. People fascinate me and everyone has a story to tell. During the nine hour drive I learned a lot about our capable driver, Michael Scully and made sure on my return journey he was the designated driver. I was curious how he routinely drove what at first appeared to be a boring empty highway. His cheerful response, "It's always an adventure."

The eldest of eighteen children, born and raised in St. Lucia of Irish descendants, Michael Scully was poorer than a church mouse, a bare foot boy with cheek he never wore shoes until he was eight years of age.

At that tender age he was responsible and cared for each sibling as they entered this world. The essence, duty and devotion to his expanding family determined his noble character. After high school he ventured to Canada to seek his fortune, was hired by Greyhound and worked unflaggingly earning his way and graduating from the University of Toronto.

A valued employee he was offered a management position and after many years of corporate life returned to the open road as a senior driver. During our brief conversations he explained the fascinating history of the Greyhound Bus Line who he has served with dedication and loyalty for almost half a century.

Michael married his high school sweetheart and they produced five children and adopted a young St. Lucian boy. All of their children graduated college and lead successful careers.

Michael is part of the Greyhound's legacy. Never distracted his capable mind and hands steered his land bound ship as gracefully as an ice skater. His unruffled persona greeted each and every passenger with a smile and patience no matter what culture or language.

Michael Scully has traveled the world embracing its enormous diversity of culture and food. Wherever he visited I am sure he'll be remembered for his grace, nobility, humility, integrity and lovely Irish brogue. I'll never forget him.

PROMISCUOUS PROGENIES

Victorian children were to be seen and not heard. My parents did not adhere to that premise when I was born in 1932. However, strict rules applied; impertinence and unruly behavior was unacceptable. Physical punishment did not exist, only a raised eyebrow and a verbal warning.

The pacifistic, polite society in which I spent my earliest years disappeared overnight on September 3, 1939. Chaos ensued with gas masks, sirens, blackout and the Blitz. Fearful parents evacuated their children to the safety of the country and often into the arms of abusive strangers.

Pre-war our polite, pacifistic society was controlled by an insidious class system devised to suppress a subservient working class. As all hell broke loose the class system was buried.

A six year roller coaster ride finally ended on VE day 1945 followed by a deep five year depression. The enemies; Germany and Japan sprang back to life aided by a generous America while Great Britain struggled to repay its debt to the Lady with the Lamp.

A grateful Great Britain warmly welcomed our brave American cousins who came to our rescue. They firmly planted their seed of independence influencing an emerging war torn generation.

We were mesmerized by Hollywood Technicolor film fantasies; glamour, fashion, slick dialogue and rags to riches happy ever after endings accomplished without a stifling, repressive 'class system'. Post war the class system once again tried to rear its ugly head and was killed by an aggressive; blossoming rebellious youth determined it would never reappear.

Pomp and Circumstance was dwarfed by the Beatles, a steady diet of violent movies, raucous television igniting a self assured, determined pop culture. Refinement flew out the window. Benign Fred and Ginger were replaced by Fred Flintstone, Esther Williams' swimming pools dried up, Singing in the Rain' went down the drain.

A promiscuous, 'me' society had been hatched. It swept across America and the British Isles. Woodstock,, LSD, pot, 'Make love not war', produced abandoned children, sexually transmitted diseases and unstable personalities.

Janis Joplin out screeched the Rolling Stones screeching guitars as rubber lips Mick Jagger strutted and thrashed out his message, 'Can't git no satisfaction'. Pornography proliferated, Hustler hustled and Playboy bounced its Bunnies. The 'F' word flourished in tandem with a new language of slang and inarticulate speech; whatsup, ya"know, bro, gimme a high five, hey dude, yeah, yeah, ooh, ooh baby, acronyms and abbreviations.

Elocution was mocked; suggesting enunciation brought either a murderous look or the classic Italian salute. Opposing the new freedom of speech I became a silent dictator fighting an uphill battle.

Ironically I loathed Britain's class system that judged one's verbal status. Before accusing me of being a hypocrite analyze my theory; language beautifully spoken denotes communication, coarse, unintelligible babble ignites confusion.

I cringed with embarrassment for promiscuous progenies wangling a mangled plea in front of TV judges and nasal whiners dispensing television news and weather. Scratched nails on a blackboard are more acceptable than the early morning screaming meemies crowding television network plazas waving unreadable signs.

Adding insult to injury; Reality Television Housewives, Jersey Shore situations, survivors, bachelors, bachelorettes and inane sit-com laugh tracks. Television has spawned instant conversation interruption as host and guest wrangle for attention. Most importantly vital documentary narration is often drowned by loud musical sound tracks and bombastic explosions.

Destruction of the Tower of Babble is a mystery. What was the reason for scattering a monotheistic language resulting in squeaky Chinese, guttural German, impatient Spanish, harsh Arabic, erotic French, emotional Italian and hundreds of unfathomable dialects? Professor Henry Higgins I need your answer.

Communicating often with citizens of the Philippines is a pleasure. Their English is superb. Unlike other outsourced customer services, the Pilipino greets you with impeccable politeness and a sweet voice. If General McArthur were alive he would be impressed.

Having never produced a progeny, promiscuous or otherwise I am not qualified to pass judgment however, I am allowed an opinion and would have followed my mother's principles.

Poor as a church mouse, patience and eloquence were her assets. She did not resort to the Victorian axiom. Instead she encouraged my sister and me to engage politely in conversations and instilled the beauty of the English langue to be clearly spoken.

Her lessons served me well; I have recorded radio and television commercials, engaged in public speaking and discovered my calm, concise modulated voice solves a myriad of problems. My parents and beautiful sister are no longer here to exchange dialogue however; their voices joyfully reverberate in my memory bank

The old adage, 'Think before you speak' is not only wise about the accusatory words you may utter but conveys a tonal message whether your speech is strident, harsh, warm or mellow. Remember the beautifully spoken word is as soothing as Debussy's 'L'Après-Midi d'un Faune'.

UPPER & LOWER CASES

E-mail geeks define UPPER CASE text reflects ANGER! On board a ship I would be angry if I didn't get the lower berth as opposed to the UPPER with its creaky ladder.

Unheeded was my capital suggestion directed to the creators of a highly popular British television series depicting the UPPER and lower classes of Edwardian England;

UPSTAIRS—DOWNSTAIRS

Should have been titled

UPPER STAIRS and lower stairs.

Words such as case and suit intrigues me because they have many definitions: Case in point; my suitcase when stolen allowed me to file a lawsuit and I won my case.

So whether you case the joint, lower your eyes or have an UPPER hand don't go into a coma over a comma.

Footnote:

I have written extensively about Britain's insidious class system in both my published autobiographies;

Keep Your Pecker Up and Brief Encounters.

RAIN

I grew up in the land of rain, grey, cold and damp. That's why Mary Poppins with her 'brolly' descended to cheer us up and sprinkle a teaspoonful of her magical sugar over our magnificent gardens to ensure they were the envy of the world.

London rain was not the steamy, humidity of the tropical Rain Forest or the monsoons that drove Joan Crawford insane in 'Rain'. London rain prevented us from wearing white. Our rain drops burgeoned with soot from all the chimneys Mary's boyfriend tried to keep clean. Dirty raindrops were not visible on our drab black and brown clothing.

The season of our malcontent had begun. Burberry's became famous for their raingear; 'Macintoshes' aka 'Macs'. Thanks to the Duke of Wellington our feet were kept dry.

A genius rubber manufacturer studying the Duke's handsome, calf hugging leather boots created a water proof loose fitting version, we gleefully nicknamed, 'Wellies'.

In conjunction with the he Duke's boots his famous, victorious 'Battle of Waterloo' applied to anything wet; water., essential in beer production and flushing toilets known in England as the 'Loo'

Ensuring the Duke's supreme effort never forgotten, wayward perpetrators of dastardly deeds were warned, 'Be prepared to meet your Waterloo'—translated; injury or death!

Following the grey of winter, one could sense a rebirth as promised by Robert Browning's poetic quote, 'Oh to be in England now that spring is here'. A soft roll of thunder, a rustling breeze alerted one to observe crocuses, violets and daffodils bursting from their hibernation.

For a few lovely weeks in summer females in pretty frocks blossomed like our beauteous gardens and the male species strutted in cricket white trousers, striped blazers and straw boaters;, a fleeting Manet scenario.

Smoky autumn arrived, stripping leaves exposing squirrels gathering their harvest. Branches, black and barren blended with the ubiquitous English symbol of inclement weather, the black 'brolly' accompanied infuriating expressions, 'Nice day for the ducks' and 'It's raining cats and dogs'.

Why blame those poor creatures for the expected, annual deluge? Why not 'Pennies from Heaven or Violets'

Why Gene Kelly and his epic, 'Singing in the Rain' didn't choose London as his location is a mystery? He painted Paris as his American in Europe utopia and ignored our little island set in a silver sea?

Had he forgotten we were glorious and victorious defeating the Spanish Armada and Hitler? Maybe Gene couldn't fathom why we were unable to conquer the annual invasion of the 'black brollys'. Trust me we huddled shivering masses didn't splash gleefully in puddles Singing and Dancing in the Rain.'

THE MYSTERY OF YA'KNOW VERY WELL

Professor Henry Higgins didn't know his ass from his elbow when he demanded, "Why can't the English teach their children how to speak?" Poor Eliza Doolittle was driven to distraction with his 'words, words, words.

Surely the professor was referring to dialect and elocution and not adverbs, adjectives, dangling participles and predicates? No other language proffers a mangled, convoluted, confusing grammatical mess, only the English.

English is my native tongue, born and raised in London, England I learned to 'speak' beautifully. My diction and modulated tones were perfect. However, grammar was a nightmare, worse than algebra and calculus.

The confusion began when the headmaster at school sternly announced, "Very well, you are to be punished". My trembling outstretched palm awaited the sting of his lethal cane. My crime; an outburst of inappropriate laughter during class.

Two days later I received verbal praise, "Very well done indeed" when my landscape oil painting was prominently displayed in the school's main corridor. I knew then I wanted to become an artist and banished the inane, meaningless, annoying words, 'very well' from my vocabulary.

Amusingly, a doctor from India who sounded like Peter Sellers impersonating him caused me to laugh uncontrollably when he diagnosed my condition as 'Very very serious and no laughing matter'.

Following the laughter, I paid little attention to verbal insouciance until visually impaired, unable to read or drive, my freedom was curtailed. Unwillingly, television became a vital resource.

My remote control received a Jane Fonda work out surfing channels in search of intelligence. Unrelenting diatribe delivered by irritating voices and explosive commercials assaulted my ears. Eliza confronted Henry Higgins, my television set did not respond.

Only my beloved, beautiful music collection soothed my savage breast. A restless creature, constantly seeking information and knowledge, I tried to ignore the silent, staring grey glass eye of the infamous 'tube'.

Stare no more grey eye, I am in control with the power of remote 'zap' and have created a television game plan; selective programming and players whom I can eliminate with my thumb.

A variety of excellent programs proved satisfying. Then I became fascinated and mystified listening to articulate, educated players freely spew and toss 'very and well', the insouciance, words banished from my childhood verbiage. I didn't zap, I kept score.

Hot to trot with my game, I was determined to get to the 'very bottom of the well' syndrome. Were the players not feeling well, fallen into a well or drilling for oil? Why had adjectives disappeared from their throats and been replaced with 'very'?

The 'two' most overused word mystery began to unravel. Obviously, a hesitant 'well' stalled an immediate answer and the ubiquitous 'very', simplistic laziness.

Game over until, glitzy celebrities and bumbling, mumbling millionaire athletes, (who could afford a language coach) dominated the glass eye with their unending, "ya'know's."

No, I do not know what the hell they knew. Bristling with annoyance I scoured the 2012 lists of 'most over used words.' Very, well and ya'know' were nowhere to be found! Were the 'Word Experts' deaf?

My questioning received apathy and chastisement, "Get a life, Higgins is old hat and frankly my dear no one gives a damn!"

Be assured, insouciant, moronic Moriarty this Sherlock is on the case and will not rest until the mystery of Ya'know Very Well is solved.

IGNORED

During the era of Tsars and Scarlet O'Hara
if your dance card was empty you were
classified as a wallflower'—a sweet name
for being shy and ignored.

Today in our electronic crazed age there
Are millions of 'wallflowers' ignored by
Corporate America. We shrinking violets,
who are visually impaired, disabled and
Seniors do not have access to the ultimate,
necessary communication device known
as the Internet and E-Mail.

It is more than annoying and frustrating,,
it is unconscionable. A telephone call is
greeted with raucous music, 'prompts' and
robotic recorded voices. Speaking to a
human being is akin to finding a needle in
a haystack.

An old fashion letter is discarded to the waste basket. No wonder the US Postal Service is bankrupt.

Culturally we have slipped into a hypnotic warp; a fast paced steady diet of slick television dialogue, acronyms and apathy accompanied by gunfire and foul language.

Wallflowers unite! Wave your petals, stems and leaves and speak up. Help me to Wake Up America, its population, corporations and institutions.

Don't ignore the warning signs before we return to caves and grunts.

THE FINAL JOURNEY

No accolades when I die
Please, I beg you do not cry
Departing Planet Earth
my residence since birth
for a wondrous adventure
in the infinite universe
A new location, a better place
meeting my Creator face to face
greeting friends and family
flowing with love and harmony
Secure tranquility
promised for eternity
where I pray you'll be
joining me